A Guide to Promoting a Positive Classroom Environment

A Guide to Promoting a Positive Classroom Environment

Umesh Sharma
Monash University, Australia

John Roodenburg
Monash University, Australia

and

Steve Rayner
Newman University, UK

SENSE PUBLISHERS
ROTTERDAM/BOSTON/TAIPEI

A C.I.P. record for this book is available from the Library of Congress.

ISBN: 978-94-6300-341-4 (paperback)
ISBN: 978-94-6300-342-1 (hardback)
ISBN: 978-94-6300-343-8 (e-book)

Published by: Sense Publishers,
P.O. Box 21858,
3001 AW Rotterdam,
The Netherlands
https://www.sensepublishers.com/

Printed on acid-free paper

TABLE OF CONTENTS

PREFACE

This book is different. It is not a run of the mill educational text. It deliberately aims not only to provide information, but also by using a narrative that explores experience, develops knowledge and understanding that helps put 'theory' into 'practice'. Our thanks therefore go to a vast number of colleagues, characters, friends and students we have worked with in various educational settings. We think there is a great deal to learn from this story, but we also hope you will enjoy considering the many issues related to teaching, learning and professional development from what we would claim to be a new angle and a different perspective. We do hope the reading will prompt positive thinking, intelligent inclusion, and potential new practices.

ACKNOWLEDGEMENTS

We would like to acknowledge a number of colleagues and family members who assisted us with various aspects of the book. The idea for the content and style was germinated by discussions with a number of our graduate students who said that they liked the stories we tell about different characters when teaching about challenging behaviour, asking for a book of such stories. Thank you all for igniting the idea: real life stories to bring theory to life.

We thank the many real people who shared their life experiences with us; who in so doing have helped our personal and professional formation, and now provide material to ground our writing. It is their challenges that made us think of ways such challenges could be effectively addressed by sound theory and understanding. It is their success stories that confirmed the benefits of evidence-based theories working in practice to give us a fuller picture. We thank them all, not least for enriching our lives.

There are numerous colleagues who have kindly read various drafts of the book and provided excellent ideas to improve the content and style. In particular we appreciated the comprehensive feedback and editing provided by Dr. Esther Roodenburg, and review of every-day readability by Mrs Esma Job.

We would also like to thank our immediate families.

From Umesh: Shivum thank you for sharing your stories from your classroom, playground and school. Your stories really helped me. Shipra thanks for listening to my ideas when I was writing the book. You were a very good listener and provided a very useful perspective of a parent. You were also highly patient – Thank you.

From John: Warmest appreciation to Esther my wife for patience, encouragement, and lifelong shared experiences with wonderful collegial discussions.

From Steve: Eileen for unfailing belief, support and understanding. And letting me visit Australia and work with colleagues at Monash University.

We would also like to thank Sense (particularly Peter de Liefde) who agreed to publish this book. The narrative style for this type of book is still gaining ground, and we appreciate Sense's openness to innovation. You were so prompt in responding and agreed to publish this book – Thank you very much.

THE JOURNEY

Learning Teaching on the Road

OVERVIEW AND KEY CONCEPTS

- Introduction: Reading this book
- Understanding and experience: Stories, perspectives and practice
- Principles into practice: Creating positive learning environments
- Why contribute to creating a positive learning environment?

INTRODUCTION: WHY READ THIS BOOK?

This book explores thinking about teaching and learning as an educative process. It is about creating a positive learning environment for positive learning, teaching, personal, and professional growth. The book is not about developing subject-based expertise as a teacher in a specific area of knowledge content. The need for work in subject-based development is for another book. Instead, we focus here on the premise that teaching is not only the transmission of knowledge. It is a process that also encompasses experiences, skills, understanding, attitudes and participation as a teacher engages in teaching people.

Questions for reflection

Having browsed the title, the table of contents and the overview above, list your expectations–what do you most hope to gain from reading it?

Reading this book might usefully be likened to taking a journey. We hope the reader – you – will find the experience of reading this book one that is both enjoyable and worthwhile. The guess is you are an educational practitioner: a newly qualified teacher; perhaps a senior teacher; or maybe a school leader; or even a university or college student or lecturer involved in an educational programme of study.

We certainly expect you to be interested in learning. What we hope to do is to convince you that learning, teaching and education are all a process that is much like a journey. It is a 'never ending' journey that offers a great deal in terms of hope, aspiration, affirmation and fulfilment. The satisfaction of playing a lead role in facilitating the growth and development of individuals and their community during this journey is widely acknowledged by educationists as one of the greatest feelings experienced and a reward that makes the job so very worthwhile.

Usually a planned journey, let us say, an 'east to west coast' road trip, has a distinct beginning and end, but then a different journey may not be such a straightforward 'get on and get off' experience. It may also involve seeing new places, meeting new people, hearing new voices, discovering new ideas and well, all in all, taking detours, deciding on new directions, making choices that like it or not will involve learning! We would like to suggest that you might approach reading this book like an unplanned road trip, open to new challenges and learning experiences.

Please do not expect to get a 'how to do it' manual with lots of bulleted lists, steps, ingredients, and claims for a one stop teaching handbook. Instead, we hope to help you think through what it means to teach; to reflect upon the ways in which we share and collaborate to learn; and, also to help you realize how important individual contributions are to the success of a learning community. And in all of this, we believe, much depends upon how you personally approach the journey.

A career in education is arguably very much like a longer version of this same kind of journey or perhaps we can call it a road trip. It is to some extent reflected in a set of themes described by Pirsig as a way of learning and knowing in 'Zen and The Art of Motorcycle Maintenance'. Pirsig (1974) writes,

> The *classical* mode proceeds by reason and by laws. The classic style is straightforward, unadorned, unemotional, economical and carefully proportioned. Its purpose is to bring order out of chaos. The *romantic* mode is primarily inspirational, imaginative, creative, and intuitive. Feelings rather than facts predominate. Motorcycle riding is romantic while motorcycle maintenance is purely classic. (pp. 70–71)

But this is where the analogy stops: we believe there are more modes than two in our approach to 'learning teaching on the road'. The taking of this journey is complex by its nature, frustrating at times, yet full of the potential for deep and intense rewards in the form of personal satisfaction and fulfilment. The message we wish to share with you in this book is therefore the importance of being positive, and using this aspect of *personal psychology* as a key resource in making the trip work well for you and for everyone else you involve in the experience.

To bring what is often presented as dry theory to life, and to illustrate practice, the book is presented as a narrative involving several characters in different stages of the teaching trip. The cast for this story is listed at the beginning of each chapter, so for example includes Fred, a school Principal taking on a new school in his first term. Then there is Kate, a newly qualified teacher starting out in her teaching career. And there are others, including teachers with specific posts of responsibility, and other 'stakeholders' in the school community, such as an Educational Psychologist, teaching assistants, parents, and a member of the school council.

These characters, drawn from real life, offer a way for us to present a continuing series of perspectives, voices expressing points of view, and in so doing tell a story that reflects individual contributions to the work of the school community. These form part of what we mean to show is a complex and continuing activity in growing and maintaining a positive learning environment. Call-out boxed allow for focus and reflection.

UNDERSTANDING AND EXPERIENCE: STORIES, PERSPECTIVES AND PRACTICE

Let us get back to the idea of a journey. The first thing to realize is the trip is going to involve arrival in a new place, getting to know people, and establishing what goes on in the daily routines of the organization. Then there are the hidden aspects of community life, less easily perceived yet equally important. These include aspects of the organizational culture in the school community, reflecting values, beliefs and attitudes; many of which will be deeply embedded in the ethos of the school, and some may not accurately reflect the more formal rules, regulations and official policy of the institution.

Every stop off along the road trip requires moving through this process of making a start. A great deal of it will draw upon tacit knowledge. This involves finding out about people; where is the best place to get X and to whom do you go to get Y; and most importantly when you have an issue, where you can find some help in sorting it out. Beneath this surface level of tacit knowledge is a second level of human inter-personal knowledge. Here the work takes on more complexity as you learn who you agree with, who you can trust or work well with, and to know those you need to tread with more carefully. And then there is the all-important management of classroom and staff-student relationships running through the school week and academic year. It is the kind of knowledge that is rarely documented in the ring-binder manual on how to do teaching. But it actually forms the most important, sometimes stressful, and oft most rewarding part of the on the road teaching trip.

To sum up: the idea behind the narrative structure of this book is in part to access some of this hidden area of the 'learning community'. We therefore aim in some sense to create a learning experience in the telling of the story. It is all about moving toward a greater level of understanding and experience, and we think this can be achieved by paying attention to a series of accounts that describe different perspectives and practices, all drawn from the real experiences of the authors. To this end, we include prompts, sign-posts and indicators high-lighting key issues, concepts and aspects of the theory under-pinning the practice related in the story. We then set out to introduce the context within which practitioner development remains a continuing process: this involves structure, knowledge, expertise and professional learning. This work or 'agency' reflects the synthesis and use of theory in developing practice, producing a new knowledge that we recognise as praxis. The sum total of this synthesis of professional learning and knowledge, that is the running balance of these actions and outcomes, is *praxis*. Put simply, praxis is both process and knowledge that is a combination of *theory* and *practice*. And of course such theory relies upon well-validated evidence-based theory, blended appropriately in a professional context, reflecting experience, and thereby contributes to ensuring efficacy in practice.

We should add that Bernstein, a leading sociologist and educationist, once stated that in praxis there can be no prior knowledge of the right means by which we can realize the end in a particular situation, since this is only finally specified in deliberating about the means appropriate to a particular situation (Bernstein, 1983: 147). In other words, we are always learning in teaching, and as a professional practitioner, each year brings with it a different student cohort(s), with new challenges and a fresh start; each week a new set of priorities, and each lesson, the great unknown. We also learn a great deal of this expertise by either listening to peers or noticing how something is actually practiced. More complexity unfolds however, as we think about what we want to achieve, we reconsider the best way we might reach that desired objective. Teaching and learning for different individuals, and when considered within a community, are not straightforward concepts easily converted to metrics or even to a goals-based approach in managing a programme of study. Moreover, the effect of the context within which we find ourselves will add to the complexity of the work involved in teaching and learning. This is reflected in the way in which a wide range of differences and diversity form the basis of the school community, and so mirrors the way in which learning is at the same time always deeply personal, mostly social, and invariably organizational in its implications for the journey.

PRINCIPLES INTO PRACTICE: CREATING POSITIVE LEARNING ENVIRONMENTS

The theory behind our approach to learning and teaching in this book is largely drawn from several areas of educational psychology. These include humanistic psychology (Maslow, 1954; Rogers, 1969); positive psychology (Csikszentmihalyi, 1990; Peterson & Seligman, 2004; Robbins, 2008); individual differences and dispositional psychology (Galton, 1865; Riding & Rayner, 2000; Zhang, Sternberg & Rayner, 2012); educational leadership (Rayner 2009; Shields, 2011); pedagogy (Zeichner & Liston, 1996), inclusive education (Mastropieri & Scruggs, 2010;

Rayner, 2007; Sharma & Loreman, 2014) and teacher education (Sharma & Nuttall, 2015; Sharma, Simi, & Forlin, 2015).

Humanistic psychology includes a set of ideas about motivation and the need to maintain a healthy approach to life as an individual. To be mentally healthy, individuals must take personal responsibility for their actions, regardless of whether those actions are positive or negative. An individual's potential and the importance of growth and self-actualization form part of a person-centered explanation for human behaviour that is grounded in the notion of a natural desire for growth and development. One fundamental belief of humanistic psychology held by some is that people are innately good, with mental and social problems resulting from deviations from this natural tendency, though some would disagree with this philosophical position, while holding other humanistic values of individual worth.

The second and major psychological influence in the approach to learning and teaching in this book is the area of positive psychology. This is an approach that seeks to understand positive emotions such as joy, optimism and contentment. Positive psychology is interested in the conditions that allow individuals, groups and organizations to flourish. There are several key constructs in this theory that are immediately relevant to the task of building a positive learning environment. These include well-being, fulfillment, happiness, affirmation, engagement, mindfulness, and perhaps most importantly, the ability to find meaning in everyday life, work and play. For our purposes here, so much of this recently developing branch of psychology can be applied to the stories of 'travelers' journeying on the learning-teaching road trip.

The psychology of Individual Differences also provides a range of theories and assessments which can be used to tell us how a student or indeed how any colleague will typically approach a task, or tackle a learning problem, each having a set of preferences for thinking, socializing and interpreting the world around them. This approach includes key variables and constructs drawn from the domains of personality, intelligence, sex, ability, as well as other constructs more closely linked to performance in learning, such as cognitive style, learning styles, meta-cognition, motivation and self-perception as a learner. The theory is particularly relevant as a major contributor to shaping tacit (most often unspoken) knowledge and related ways in which a school community will manage its educational diversity – personal, social and organizational.

A theory of educational leadership is extremely diverse and for our purposes here, we draw upon some particular theories of inclusive, transformative and distributed leadership. These in turn are used to introduce new ideas for organizing practice, clustered around the concepts of 'intelligent inclusion', 'positive behaviour', and an 'integrative form of educational management'. Similarly, and implicitly, a theory of pedagogy is adopted to establish a pragmatic approach, describing the part played by action-based participatory professional development in leading to the idea of combining reflective practice with research–led and evidence-based information.

This approach presumes that theory can inform practice (and indeed the reverse) in ways that support, enable, and ensure continuing professional learning.

For those who like to dig a little deeper, the idea of journeying on a road trip in this book is also influenced by an understanding of a constructivist basis to learning, subject in turn to epistemic beliefs that more generally influence approaches to thinking and learning, for example the Epistemological Reflection Model (see Baxter Magolda, 2004). This framework pre-supposes several levels of learning, moving from an initial stage of passively receiving and conceiving knowledge in an absolute way as right or wrong, along a progression toward a relative perception of knowledge as a point of view, and then on to beginning to perceive knowledge as correct relative to various contexts. Finally, at the highest level, the learner begins to realize multiple possibilities for knowledge and the need for knowledge claims to be evaluated, set against the quality of the argument and evidence provided. The design of curricula and construction of study programmes of represent an important aspect of pedagogy and mirror the way in which we propose what theories of learning and thinking should be applied to the continuing development of professional learning and applied practice. Crucially, personal and professional values and/or beliefs reflect a moral basis for this development over time.

The over-riding intention throughout our book is therefore to draw upon notions of resilience, well-being, transformative leadership, and inclusive education, to inform evolving conceptions, explanations and the management of practitioner development contributing to positive learning in a school community. We aim to further shape the idea of a 'reflective practitioner' evolving into a 'thinking practitioner'. Such practitioners are conceived to be professionals who will be engaged in leading the learning, while managing a continuing and worthwhile contribution to the educational community to which they belong.

Some of the key features in this approach, involve a number of different ideas and applications of theory such as Positive Behaviour Support including:

- Reflective teaching.
- Well being and self-confidence.
- Personal motivation.
- Intelligent inclusion.
- Transformative leadership.

Chapters 2 to 4 deal with the underlying psychology for developing positive school cultures. The section introduces the narrative approach of the book: real life experiences told through fictional practitioners telling their story of improving practice while continuing to contribute to the learning organization or community in which they work. The characters provide exemplars of teachers at the coalface humanizing education in finding ways of effectively building positive inclusive relationships marked by trust, collaboration, self-efficacy, independence, and engagement.

Chapters 5 to 7 of the book deal with ideas and ideals, recognizing the role of beliefs, and putting evidence-based theory into practice for developing a positive school community. This section deals with the wider issues relevant to managing the whole school. It provides an account of leadership distributed throughout the learning community. It also gives consideration to the nature of the benefits that a positive approach to learning and teaching can bring to everyone in the school community. This includes the students, the work force and the wider community. The focus for the reader, however, remains on the individual's personal contribution to all of these areas as an important member of the learning community. The recurring theme running through this story and our main message for the reader is to emphasize the place of reflection and thinking about practice. To put it more theoretically, this takes us to the highest level of epistemic development identified earlier in a description of the 'Epistemological Reflection Model': that is, evaluativism/objectivism–subjectivism (see Muis, 2007). If we refer again to the idea of journeying along the road trip, it is like learning how to drive and quite crucially, remembering to use the rear view mirror. The driver makes full use of the reflection, aware of what has passed, in order to take decisions about the present, so that the journey may continue, and a destination at some point in the near future, be safely reached.

As expected in any journey, we sincerely hope this book will not be boring, but rather that you will actually enjoy the trip. For most of us the trip is the most enjoyable where we can watch, socialize and learn from others. By using a narrative approach in this book, we hope that dry theory still comes along, but in the back seat.

ENABLING INCLUSIVE LEARNING INTERVENTIONS

OVERVIEW AND KEY CONCEPTS

- Wellbeing
- Stress and Individual Differences
- Problem Ownership
- Intelligent Inclusion
- Diagnostics beyond classification and labelling

Meet the Cast

Main Characters:

Kate – Teacher, newly appointed as principal of rural three-teacher school
Mary – An experienced teacher, working at Kate's school for a long time.
Nick – School Psychologist

Minor Characters:

Robert – Junior teacher at Kate's school
Stan – Teacher at a neighbourhood school

WELLBEING

As Kate rounded the corner in her small car, wipers working furiously, she braked hard so as not to plough into the herd of jerseys that were lazily crossing the road from milking. She watched the dairy farmer in the sleet following close behind the herd on his four-wheel motorbike. As she waited she pondered how different this was from the previous 10 years, travelling to her western suburbs school through busy and impatient traffic. Here, now in a lush valley with snow-capped mountains in the distance, time or rather timelessness and community seemed to be worlds apart from her previous experience. At first the 23 km distance from the house she rented in the town to the three teacher rural school seemed a long way, but then, she didn't want to live by herself in a house down a lonely country lane, and she soon realised that it took her half the time to travel the 23 km than it had taken her to travel half the distance to her previous school in the city.

9

There had been lots of adjustments in the last six months: new social networks in town, the new community surrounding the school, the role of principal of a small school, composite classes, and yes, finding herself the one to make the final decisions. Why, only last week when the school toilets all failed, the regional office had told her it was her decision as to whether she needed to close the school! In a new context with so many changes, she was also wrestling with the notion of leadership and management. It felt as though no one had prepared her for it. All of this was on top of a full-time teaching load and an empty house to go home to. The pace of country life might seem to be easy-going and slow, but with school council meetings, parent meetings, mid year reports, well, she had hardly had any time to go back to Melbourne and relax with friends.

As the last cow cleared the road and the farmer waved, Kate recalled the excitement she had felt when she had received news of her appointment. She recalled how easy the first few days had seemed. The kids all settled down so quickly. The older ones looked after the younger ones. The parents had been so welcoming. The only initial reservation she had felt was about the other two teachers. Mary had been at the school at 27 years and her territory was well staked out: having taught grades 3 and 4 for most of this time, she remained with this level. Robert was on a one-year contract fresh from university, and although enthusiastic, he made it quite clear he really wanted to be back in the city. Come Friday 3.30pm and he was on the road, only to drive back on Monday mornings. Kate had never taught classes below grade 4, but on hearing from the school council members that they were very excited to have a man to teach their footballing boys in grade five, she thought it only sensible to allocate herself the junior grades. It didn't take long to realise that with ten of her class being prep children, it wasn't easy to leave the classroom to attend to principal's duties, but at least there were no behaviour problems.

Questions for reflection

1. Identify stressors in your professional and personal life – and how do you handle them?

2. Would others describe you as authoritarian or consultative, or somewhere in between?

3. Do you share your dilemmas with friends or keep silent ?

There were some clear advantages in driving the beautiful country road to school. It gave Kate time to think. She seemed to be more easily irritated than she ever had been with the more difficult children of the western suburbs. Yes, she was increasingly more organised, more directive, and perhaps more authoritarian. But as she drew up at the school, a couple were waiting for her, giving her only enough time to squelch the minor pang of guilt that such a dictatorial management was warranted by a need to cope with so much that was expected of her.

THE STRESS OF INDIVIDUAL DIFFERENCES

The couple seemed a little uncomfortable and it soon became clear why. They had moved up to an inexpensive rental house on one of the local farms. They hoped to pick up local seasonal farm labouring and domestic work. They had three children they were wanting to enrol, a boy in grade six who suffered from Asperger's, and twins in grade 1 who both had learning difficulties: Kate only later found out these were associated with foetal alcohol syndrome. As Kate completed the enrolment formalities the next day, she made a decision: it was time to stop being the self-effacing idealist. Inclusion was all fair and well, but if she were to survive she would need to morph into a Sergeant Major, which left her wondering about her decision to enrol the kids. Over lunch, Robert chewed her ear about the new boy in his class. What could be done to get more help, and how long would it take to get someone to support him? After all he'd had a teacher's aide at the previous school! He said he was only just surviving, and as for a kid with a mental condition, well, he didn't have a clue. With the thought that she didn't need any more drain on her time, having already had to provide more support for this problem than she really had time for, and pondering what Rob *had* learnt in his course at university, Kate decided to telephone the regional office.

She now started to wonder about the twins in her class; they appeared, well, fairly docile now, but what was she in for? Why on earth weren't these kids properly assessed and placed in facilities where they would get the help they needed, she pondered. "Realism," she thought, "get real Kate," she told herself: "just a silly romantic dream, a stress free life under the shadow of snow peaked mountains, oh yea? Not such worlds apart after all."

The regional office put her through to the school psychologist. Nick would be out in two weeks.

PROBLEM OWNERSHIP

"Two weeks...surely next week at least? Is there no earlier time?" She tried to keep the distress out of her voice. "This is really urgent. I may have a teacher going off on stress leave. Besides, we have a duty of care and there may be things we need to know that we currently don't. And the two in my room, well I need to know fast, before other parents start to complain...."

Nick asked her to send the children's' details so he could check if there were any files. He asked a series of questions, and on assessing the situation, the best he could do was give some interim pointers. While he could not manage to come out for a couple of weeks, he also offered to talk with Rob over the phone. Finally, they set up for Rob to go in to talk with Nick the next evening around six.

Kate felt some relief, but frustrated that even with Nick's support, she would probably have to wait quite a few months if not a year before she could expect any real assistance. She found herself rather hoping that the two kids with learning difficulties in her class could be identified as having an identifiable condition sufficient to warrant a teacher aide. Yes, she thought, come what may, she was determined to get a teacher aide!

That evening she rang Stan at the school up the road. Stan had some fragile X kids, and seemed to know how to get resources. The discussion was very useful. Stan had managed to get quite a few resources and pointed her to a number of ways of getting them.

"But," he warned, "you must get an assessment and be careful, they will do anything to find an excuse to cut your entitlements. Last year the Ed Psychs told me they thought the disabled kids in my school were over-resourced and that too much individual attention was detrimental for them! They have no idea." Kate appreciated the discussion: to be forewarned was to be prepared, and now she was ready for a fight.

Despite having given Rob some materials, and the promised follow up phone calls from Nick, Kate was relieved when the day finally arrived for Nick's visit. She was well rehearsed with every possible argument as to why they needed a teacher's aide, and urgently. She had organised for her class to be distributed across the other two rooms so that she had the morning free to talk with Nick. After brief pleasantries and some coffee, Kate sat down with Nick in the small staffroom. Nick looked out of the window that framed the mountains, still snow capped in the distance, and commented on the beauty of the drive down the valley to the school. But Kate was in no mood for the positive talk. With three weeks full of cogitating concern, she was ready to get on with business. Arms folded she asked:

"So, what extra help do you have to offer us for ensuring we can meet the needs of these three at-risk disabled children?"

Nick sensed that he was being handed the problem, but he wanted to work together, so he acknowledged Kate's stress.

"Yea, such kids can be really stressful – eating up our time. Before we move on, I would like to know how you have been going with them."

In the process of Nick's attentive listening and seeming understanding, Kate found herself outlining her concerns of the last three weeks. Nick was a good listener. Trying to appear professional, she carefully tried to make the most of various frustrations and incidents, while working hard to sound caring, competent and conscientious.

"It sounds like you are doing all the right things."

Kate's heart sank. She wanted extra resources. Had she sounded too competent? Had he not heard the frustrations?

"Look, well may we be coping, but only just, and it isn't without a considerable cost in time and effort, taking away valuable time from other kids. And I have to spend a lot of time with Rob. And even now, here I am away from all the other kids having to take time out talking here because of them." Kate's voice had risen and there was clear frustration in her voice. "The bottom line really is: What can *you* do to help us get a teacher's aid?" There. She had him. She had come to the point, no soft talking.

But Nick still did not engage with her challenge. "This is very frustrating for you. I do understand."

Kate wanted to challenge him about how someone from a comfortable office who could choose his time in coming out had *any* idea, but she kept her cool to hear him continue:

"Believe you me, I know how tough it can be. It throws me back to my days as a rural school head teacher when freshly out of Uni. I had twenty seven kids including a hearing impaired kid all on my own! and it was twelve months before they appointed a rural school aide, who came in for three days a week."

That was him *then*, Kate thought, but this is about me *now!* Nevertheless, here she was talking to a colleague. She was curious.

"So, you are a teacher – you taught in a rural school – where was that?" There ensued a frank exchange and sharing of the joys and frustrations of teaching in a rural community and at a small school. Nick knew intuitively how sharing feelings associated with common experiences facilitates trust. Trust was slowly taking over from all the mistrust that had been generated in the discussions with Stan. Nick sensed that Kate's veiled hostility was ebbing. But, he knew, returning to the point of stress would require sensitivity and an unconditional appreciation for Kate's dilemmas.

He recognised and reminded himself of the underlying issue of problem ownership. He recognised the potentially destructive scenario: if *he* accepted responsibility for the problem, the next step would carry considerable pressure to capitulate to her pre-determined solution of a teacher's aide. He needed to establish genuine trust, at least enough to allow for an introduction of cooperative problem solving. It required genuineness in the context of what Carl Rogers had established as unconditional positive regard and understanding: only then could they move from what Nick perceived as a somewhat adversarial position to cooperate in "ganging up" on what he regarded was really Kate's problem. Only then, if she felt ownership *and* Nick's genuine concern and support, was there any hope for getting Kate to think in a broader context beyond immediate practical wants and/or solutions. To do this meant talking about inclusion in the broader sense before he did any assessment work with the students. It was, he believed, such an important part of getting effective professional development: on the job coaching.

Questions for reflection

What resources are available to you for professional mentoring or coaching, and what use do you make of them?

INTELLIGENT INCLUSION

But Nick also knew that the field was ever changing, and he hoped this change meant effective advancement. Having gone through the integration initiatives, on to the inclusion imperatives articulated over the last two decades, he was now old enough to realise an enduring dilemma: in practicality, no clearly established point of arrival had been achieved, though for some this had been resolved by declaring that inclusion is about process, the journey, and that's it. But so what? Journeys go places!

A recent discussion with a visiting scholar, Steve Rayner from the UK, to the University in Melbourne, now came to mind. Steve, in conversation, had suggested that essentially, the academic debate over inclusion remains locked in an argument over ideals (albeit generally accepted as laudable) and imperfect or impossible practice. Some practitioners, he'd pointed out, claim to practice inclusive education, others social inclusion, yet when closely examined, such practice still reflect the very powerful tensions, contradictions and dilemmas posed by implementing an ideal.

Nick had enjoyed the intellectual stimulation of the academic debate Rayner had pointed to: less public, however, and yet still equally relevant to this attempt at revising and refining our ideas of what is inclusive education, Nick thought, was the theoretical debate reflecting differences people adopted in terms of ontology (what one knows) and epistemology (how one knows). Much of this surrounded notions of equity, fair play, discrimination and say, positions held by some who argue any affirmative intervention is unfair. Rayner had suggested that the underpinning argument in this debate is both ideological and moral: it involves asking fundamental questions about education, its purpose, its implementation, and a belief in what it is to be human. And behind this debate again lie yet deeper questions about the nature of the human being and the worlds s/he inhabits as an individual and also as a member of any social group(s). These issues needed to be considered in terms of pedagogic, philosophical, sociological and psychological aspects of practice. A lot of necessary debate and integrative work yet to be done, but how could he hope to begin to share this with Kate who simply wanted answers to what she perceived as her immediate needs? How, pondered Nick, could he get her to see these within the perspectives of a broader educational, interdisciplinary context?

As Nick understood it, Steve Rayner had suggested making a start with 'intelligent inclusion' as an idea. This was perhaps best imagined as a conceptual framework: it strives for a pragmatic approach to the learner and learning in an integrative way, synthesising new and old ideas. It posits the notion of an educative process that reflects a seasonal cycle of growth essentially transformative in nature. It anticipates education as an outcome that reflects an enabling and empowering experience that provides the individual and society with ways to engage in managing knowledge, for both a personal and a public 'good'. This means taking more seriously the implications of schooling and its limited resources, as located within the locale, and as a part of the wider social community. The school holds a central position in the life beat of the community.

Nick paused, recalling the following notes he'd been checking the previous evening in preparation for teaching a doctorate class due in a fortnight's time. Nick was planning to talk to the following key points about implementing what he wanted to call an 'intelligent' way of practising inclusive education. These considerations required thinking about making basic changes, that is, taking decisions and showing leadership in key aspects of re-shaping pedagogy and re-balancing the curriculum (intended and experienced), together with a new consideration of relevant aspects of educational sociology and psychology. Such change meant professional and sometimes personal movement. It would include:

1. *Pedagogic changes*

- Movement away from recent or current understandings of

  - Categories (SEN / Disability).
  - IQ based discriminatory setting / streaming classes.
  - Comprehensive mixed multi-mix classes.
  - Easy one-size fits all curricular frameworks.

- Movement toward new understandings of

  - Renewal of integration / inclusion models.
  - Learning needs.
  - Learning performance.
  - New forms of assessment & assessment-led pedagogy.

2. *Sociological changes*

- Movement away from recent or current understandings of

  - Multi-cultural models of community for social inclusion.

15

- Human Rights without Responsibilities.
- A common culture specific to the learning community.
- A new identity / culture specific to the evolving diversity in the local community.

- Movement toward

  - Inter-cultural models of community for social inclusion.
  - New conceptions of integrative / transformative culture.
  - Revisionist exploration of assents / artefacts / affiliation.
  - Revisionist exploration of accommodation / assimilation / acculturation.
  - New forms of cultural accommodation, assimilation and values clarification.

3. *Psychological changes*

- Movement away from outdated understandings of

  - Intelligence deficit and giftedness models.
  - Motivation and/or affective resilience.
  - Unitary/categorical models of personal and social diversity / differences.
  - Unitary/categorical models of deficit diagnostics.

- Movement toward

  - Models of individuality and personal cognition.
  - Recognising individuality – Individual Differences in predispositions.
  - Current models of differential abilities.
  - Models of personality trait.
  - Positive "strengths" psychology.

- Models of situated cognition and social diversity.
- Learning differences.
- Use of capability theory.
- Integrated forms of psycho-educational assessment (authentic, ipsative and gnostic).
- New forms of assessment-led pedagogy.

This was all too much to impart to Kate at this point in time, but for Nick it was a good foundation to work from.

Nick turned to Kate and said, "You know Kate, in the 'good old days' Ed Psychs were called in to classify kids: the familiar story of labelling so we know where to put people. It came out of an age where we thought understanding meant finding the right classification for every flora and fauna. Such classification required discrimination, which gave credence to differences according to race in ways we now recognise as racism. In more subtle ways such classificatory misconceptions attracted people to pseudoscientific intellectual pursuits like phrenology and eugenics. In this way, differences are considered as deviation from the norm, and so classed as deviant, and any such deviance as 'disabilities' and 'illnesses' requiring specialist treatment. To this day, we have assessment-based processes of confirming eligibility for funding [resources] that are still based on that deficiency model, where with the best intentions, funding and resources reward and reinforce discrimination."

Intuitively, and as a result to her Education courses, Kate understood that theoretically and ideally there was something wrong with labelling, but her frustration was in translating that to the practical world.

"I know what you are getting at, Nick, but don't you think we need to be practical here: what we really need here is some resources for these kids, and I think it is discrimination if we disadvantage them by not recognising their problems and appropriately giving them a label. So, while it is all very well to be so idealistic, isn't it a matter of compromise?"

Questions for reflection

In practicality, is inclusive educational practice just too hard?

What is the difference between labelling and diagnostics?

ABILITIES AND LEARNING DIFFICULTIES: DIAGNOSTICS BEYOND CLASSIFICATION AND LABELLING

This gave Nick an opening to talk about issues he had tried to think through a lot. "As a psychologist, I've become deeply interested in an area called Individual Differences. This area principally concerns the study of abilities and personality. Many people who are worried about labelling see the study of individual differences as "the problem" – the basis on which we classify people, thereby creating the very basis of what leads to discriminating against groups of people. What I've come to realize over a period of time is that denying that we are all different in some way can be as equally harmful as classifying people. We are each unique, and the product of a remarkable interplay of a whole lot of predispositions, traits, and notions of self in relation to one another, with our environment, and with our experiences. In that sense, the study of individual differences is really the study of predispositions, and that's why it is sometimes called a dispositional psychology. If we understand our individual differences, and we accept that there really is a broad range of individual differences, and that some of these individual differences make it more difficult for some of us to adjust to the demands of the world (known as maladaptive) while other individual differences are highly adaptive, well then, we are well on the way to diagnostics rather than classification!"

Kate shrugged. "I don't really see any difference."

Nick smiled. "Well, there's a world of difference, really. In ascertainment we are simply concerned with a categorical classification of a condition, and the condition is a matter of the fact: you have it or you don't have it. If you have it, then you warrant extra resources. These resources have little relationship to the actual impact of what you have, nor do they take into account understanding the diagnostics as a basis for intervention or specifically tailoring any assistance or help. Simply having a recognized categorical disability makes you eligible. The term 'idiot' for example has its origins in 20th century medicine and psychology, as a classification indicating severe mental retardation. While we might pride ourselves on being better informed, and not using such a term as it has become a pejorative, in reality we nonetheless carry on the same thing by simply substituting specific IQs score ranges that can be less easily used as insulting discrimination. It's a little less appealing to call someone you want to insult as 'You below 70 IQ person!'

"The point is, though, that simply classifying someone like that doesn't tell us how we can support such individuals, not least because with every individual scoring 70 or below on an ability test, there are a multiplicity of other factors that come into play to help ensure their well-being and capacity for adaptation and adjustment and learning."

Nick paused before continuing. "In fact, take for example the area of intelligence research: research has been shown to have advanced more in the last decade than the preceding 100 years, so that the notion of any usefulness in a global IQ score is now seriously challenged. Kevin McGrew (2009), one of the leaders in the field has made the point that, building on a lifelong work of 3 giants in the field, R. B. Cattell, John Horn and John Carroll, the most recent developments in ability research has given us what has become known as the CHC model. In that model we now have a table of differential abilities that is equivalent to the periodic table in chemistry."

Kate in spite of herself, and somewhat irritated, interrupted. "So how is that any different from classification – just sounds to me as though it is a finer grained way of labelling" interjected Kate.

"Well, no, it's not because it helps us to *understand* how the brain is handling or not handling information: things such as working memory as distinct from say Gf: fluid abilities (general sequential reasoning, deduction and induction), Gc: crystallised abilities, (breadth of knowledge developed through learning) or say Ga: auditory processing (ability to analyse and synthesise auditory stimuli.) Understanding exactly how these abilities differ one from another within the individual (intra-individual differences) as well as in comparison to other individuals (inter-individual differences) makes for diagnostic conclusions, with direct implications for how we can accommodate such individual differences in learning."

"You mean, these accommodations involve direct advice as to how to teach or to provide appropriate allowances?"

"Yes, exactly! What's more, because we now have a decent model of abilities, there is an explosion of research around relating these to effective strategies. But ability research isn't the only area; in personality research we now better understand how different traits work. We have defined these a lot better in the last decade or so, and there are researchers looking at these neurodevelopmental predispositions in children and ways of building personal resilience to counter maladaptive traits. So, you see that far from being a sentence, by acknowledging and understanding how we are all different, we are empowered rather than sentenced. In this way, good psycho-educational assessment looks at the individual and offers a firm basis for tailoring accommodation. In an ideal world, and hopefully in the future, the allocation of extra resources would be based on resourcing with appropriate and targeted support programs, rather than being for a specific classification.

"Even now, I can use those models to help us understand your challenging kids better, and work with you to devise specific strategies and accommodations for their own personal (special) needs. This means that the diagnostics are program focused rather than resource focused. This is what we mean by assessment led pedagogy."

"Does that mean I won't get any extra resources? Where does that leave us now, because we don't live in an ideal world!" asked Kate, not sure if she really wanted to grasp what was being said, if it would lead to her being denied resources she had been looking forward to.

"No. We still need to live in the real world that suffers from the research-practice gap, and I do feel that this gap is ever widening as research is speeding up. It might mean that for the sake of social justice we play the old classificatory game. If we

Questions for reflection

Was Nick's advice to Kate effective/ useful?

Why do you think so?

Would you do something different from what Nick suggested? If yes, why?

can meet some criteria for resourcing that will enable us to better implement clearly indicated strategies and accommodations, well, then we may need to do that. The danger however will be that in accepting such classifications; we need to ensure that it does not become a life sentence. That means a pedagogical focus with a constant review of how the kids are adapting. And that makes for a far more positive classroom culture."

Kate sighed. She waited to hear what Nick wanted. There clearly was going to be a need for give and take on the part of the school, as well as the education department.

CREATING POSITIVE LEARNING ENVIRONMENTS THROUGH RELATIONAL LEADERSHIP

OVERVIEW AND KEY CONSTRUCTS

- Anatomy of conflicts
- Evidence-based change
- Problem Ownership, Control, and Effect
- Management versus Leadership: Relationship keys to positive classroom culture
- Judgement

Meet an Increased Cast

Main Characters:

> Kate – Principal / Teacher
> Mary – An experienced teacher
> Nick – School Psychologist

Minor Characters

> Robert – Junior teacher at Kate's school
> Unassertive Louise and bossy Jenny – twins and students at Kate's school
> Judy – an experienced teacher at Professional Development (PD) session: Recalcitrant
> Rebecca (Bec) – teacher at PD session: Compulsive record keeper
> Jeff – teacher at Kate's school
> Michael – teacher at PD session
> Yvette – a shy teacher at PD session

ANATOMY OF CONFLICTS

Kate was waiting for the last students to be picked up before she could lock up the school: if they were late it might help her decide. She was in two minds about going off to the district Professional Development session that was a follow up on their group curriculum day last month. In the enthusiastic afterglow of the day, it had seemed such a good idea to follow through with activities that promised to help put the theory into practice. But in the busy weeks that followed, the homework for the session had been neglected, and it wasn't something she could do at the last moment. Did she really need to go? Did it really offer her anything she needed? She reviewed her last semester's work. She felt more in control now: the classroom had become hers, a quiet orderly culture pervaded it. She reflected on a satisfying day when suddenly her attention was distracted by the last couple of girls waiting to be picked up by their mother. The twins had started squabbling and she walked over.

" What are you two up to?"

"Louise says my painting isn't good enough to give to Nana and I said that Nana always likes my pictures and she said Nana just says that 'cos that's what Nana always does."

"I did not!"

"You did so too!"

"Now, now" intervened Kate, "I am sure that Nana will love your drawing Jenny...." and turned to speak to Louise to hear her quietly mutter: "It's not a drawing, its a painting, and anyway, mine is much better."

"Louise, Jenny's painting is beautiful, and I am sure that Nana will love yours just as much. Remember: it's not about who has done the best or who is best but simply doing your best. I am sure Nana loves you both just the same...."

"Here's Mummy" Louise called out as she ran off over to the car that was pulling up. With a shrug of her shoulder, Jenny slowly followed. As the children climbed into the car, Kate heard the argument continue: "Mummy, Louise says my painting is ugly and Nana ...." The car door slammed and she heard no more.

The contented feeling that she'd had before, the self-assured pride in bringing order to the school was now replaced by a sense of frustration. How many times had she watched the twins squabble like that? Had she not noticed an increase in other children's' bickering? If it wasn't over their work, it was over their lunch. She had noted some time ago that the squabbles so often represented the same little routine, just different content. Her perception moved from a glass three-quarter full, to one a quarter empty and with it, self-criticism. Yes, she reflected, she had brought order into the small school, but there was a niggling concern as to why there was so much more squabbling.

She had been sensitized even more to the change by the recent PD workshop run by the local school psychologist: Nick had teachers reflect on why children came up to them in the playground. What did they talk about? He had suggested teachers make notes and keep a tally of their playground interactions, categorizing them, and asked teachers to bring these to the follow-up session, to use as a baseline to determine what the school or classroom culture was really like, and also to monitor change. Kate hadn't wanted more paper work though.

The suggestion had nevertheless raised her awareness of some things as she had found herself mentally keeping a rough tally. She recalled how when she first arrived, recess and lunch times were times where the kids all headed off to their favourite corners of the playground. In the first few weeks she had been surprised to find yard duty so pleasant, simply wondering around with a coffee in her hand enjoying the country air and some mental space. If anyone came up to her, it was to show her something, or offer to share something. But now, she reflected, when someone came up, it was more often than not about some dispute, or to tell tales. In fact, not only in the playground, but also in the classroom, she had noticed the change: they came to her for such trivial and annoying things.

Self doubt. Maybe it was something she was doing and the base line could help. But Kate was good at finding alternative reasons and excuses. She handled the self-doubt nicely by assuring herself the bickering was probably just due to the time of year, winter approaching and the farming community stressed by the weather. But her subconscious mind didn't allow her to switch off quite so easily. She had done enough psychology to know deep down her cunning capacity for rationalization – a very effective defence mechanism when you don't want to or know how to change. But, for the moment it worked for her.

Her sister Megan's challenge last Christmas intruded yet again. Kate had seen a couple of Meg's children squabbling outside and couldn't help intervening. "Kate, you are always the quintessential teacher; a lot of Dad in you eh?" Megan, a graphic artist, had said it with a smile, but Kate recognised this as her way of not directly confronting her sister with "Leave my children be." In fact Megan never confronted anything directly, let alone discipline her children, those unruly children who bogged into the finest food before the adults had a chance. Kate felt reasonably calm as she recalled the incident, but what hurt most was the sting in the tail: did she really have to add that part of being like her father? He had been a teacher of the old school who believed children should not be heard and preferably not seen either, except of course in their proper place. Recalling Megan's jibe also aroused the jealousy Kate had for so long felt for the way Megan had got on with their father, while Kate always felt judged. How mean of Megan! Kate prided herself that through the personal development in her teacher training she had grown to be balanced: neither too authoritarian nor too laissez-faire.

As Kate had driven away, she felt the bind in which she was trapped. A part of her wanted to justify herself and be angry with her judgmental sister. What did she know? She had led a charmed life. Another part deep down though, knew that it was she who was judgmental, and remembered that when she had needed someone most, Megan had been there for her. Did she blame her poor mood now on her sister, or did she move on to see if there might be something she needed to confront in herself? Torn between love and pride, she consciously repressed any thought that she might have a choice.

Just then she found herself pulling up at the neighbouring school, and relief at the escape it provided, quickly joined the other teachers who had come for the PD follow up. She didn't really need another coffee, but at least it gave her something to have in her hand while she wandered over to find the least obvious seat. Nick had put the chairs in a semi-circle. Three o'clock looked a good position, sufficiently off to the side, and hopefully, if she didn't make eye contact, there would be little risk of being embarrassed.

Questions for reflection

To what degree do you think you have the capacity for honest self reflection?

How open are you to being constructively self-critical, and

How informed are you in making choices for effective change?

After a ten word welcome Nick simply turned on the data projector to show a tally sheet projected onto the screen. "If this group is typical of other groups I have taken, in the pressured world we now live, I will be very happy if at least one of you has used the handouts from the PD. Most of you will be sitting where you think you will be least likely to be asked, but fear not, I'm not into motivation by guilt. No extrinsic motivation today. Instead, I hope to demonstrate the more effective alternative: the power of ownership." An embarrassed laugh of relief ran around the circle as he announced that, when Rebecca had contacted him earlier for some clarification, he had asked her if she would mind reporting her use of the tally sheet.

EVIDENCE-BASED CHANGE

Rebecca owned up to being a compulsive record keeper. "My dad is a research scientist in agronomy and from an early age we were taught to have fun recording things and looking at frequencies. When we went on holidays, we would guess how many Holdens, Fords, and Toyotas we would see, counting them as we went along. We soon learnt to investigate first so that we made an informed guess. But even then, we were often surprised how different the tally was, and had fun trying to explain. Dad quickly taught us how that was good science, and we were rarely bored. So when Nick suggested a tally sheet, well it was kinda second nature, science that could help me understand what was going on."

Kate wondered what Science had to do with classroom culture, or more precisely, in developing responsibility. A short surprised interjection from some of the teachers registered admiration and surprise. But Rebecca went on: "I didn't only record free-time interactions, but also all interactions in the classroom. I simply kept a tally sheet on a clipboard with me all the time, and I ticked each interaction as much as possible as it happened. I didn't take time for too much detail. I rated interactions with students for three weeks across four sets of columns with Check marks. The first was in one of two columns: teacher initiated or student initiated. The second in one of four columns: free time such as at recess and lunch times; formal academic like maths; informal academic like art and drama; and physical like sport and phys ed. The third set of columns indicated whether the interaction principally concerned the behavioural, affective, cognitive or physical domain. The fourth set of columns indicated the main thrust of my action: listened/affirmed, adjudicated dispute, gave command, answered question/gave information, asked question. Then there was a 'note' column which I didn't use much."

Rebecca then projected the following table of results:

Individual Interactions with one or two students, percentage by area															
	Initiated by		Time				Domain				Main Action				
	Teacher	Student	Free	Formal	Informal	Physical	Behaviour	Affective	Cognitive	Physical	Listened	Gave Info	Asked On	Adjudicated	Instruction
Ideal	50	50	25	25	25	25	20	25	50	5	20	20	40	5	15
Expected	50	50	15	35	25	25	30	20	45	5	20	30	20	10	20
Week 1	78	22	5	43	41	11	49	8	42	1	7	46	6	19	27
Week 2	74	26	11	38	38	13	47	13	37	3	14	24	14	22	26
Week 3	75	25	16	34	38	12	47	18	34	1	17	20	16	21	26

Rebecca continued, "I purposefully didn't add up my tallies and tried to get an accurate record of my current habits in the first week, wanting to get as typical a base line as possible" she went on to explain. "As you can see, I got a surprise when I did add up the results, and you can see that keeping tally changed some things over the next two weeks, but some things nowhere near as much as I would have liked. I improved on asking questions and listening, acknowledging feelings and not being so cerebral, and in interacting in free time. They are all things I have some control over and happy that in such a short time I have been able to adjust my teaching to foster more enquiring minds. I just have to maintain that. However, even though I thought I was more available, students did not initiate more interactions, and I found myself give as many instructions as usual and adjudicate more disputes than ever. I now have lots of questions about how to change those things over which I don't feel I have any control. I feel trapped in discharging my duty of care efficiently, spending so much time stopping disputes and arguments and ensuring that students, especially the ones who have self control and attention problems, have been properly instructed and warned about dangers."

Kate felt a little vindicated to hear of another teacher who took the need for discipline seriously. The theoretical ideal she reflected was all too often frustratingly different to the practicalities of reality. She wondered what answers Nick would come up with. All very good for an advisor, but what about when there needed to be workable solutions? Nick rose to his feet.

"Thanks Bec, that's really great. When I compare your sheet to the tally sheet I first did after seven years of teaching, well, you spend a lot less time disciplining than I did!"

Kate felt even better, and was encouraged to learn that Nick had teaching experience, not just theory. Maybe he had worked out something that did work. She couldn't help asking "So Nick, did you get to spend less time adjudicating, how much less and what did you do?" She wanted straight answers; direct practical 'what to dos.' Nick looked over briefly acknowledging her with a smile, but didn't answer her challenge.

"Bec, can you give us an example of one of the disputes you recently had to adjudicate?"

PROBLEM OWNERSHIP, CONTROL, AND EFFECT

"Well, there are a couple of year four boys who are always getting into squabbles. At first I used to tell them how disappointed I was and tried to explain to them how they should behave responsibly. Then, after a while I gave up talking to them because I figured they were just attention seeking, so now I just tell them to stop, and go away from each other. Sometimes they take their time, and then I give them detention. I have tried to minimize the time it takes so they don't get any more of my attention than necessary, but they just don't seem to learn. I even praise them at the end of a session when they haven't squabbled, by telling them how well they have behaved, letting them out early for recess. I can't separate them any more than I do because my class ranges from years three to six, and the two boys and a girl are the only year four students."

Other teachers were nodding knowingly, and Nick invited others to share similar scenarios. One of the teachers asked what the squabbling was about, and wanted to know if the boys were related, or how their parents got on with one another. Another wanted to know if one of the boys was brighter than the other. As teachers started raising situations where they found themselves getting frustrated with continually repeating instructions and commands to various children who just didn't seem to listen or take responsibility, Nick broke in:

"In all of these, who do you reckon has a problem?"

"These kids all have problems, problems being responsible for themselves, and behaving – just too spoilt these days" came the immediate response from one of the older teachers. But it wasn't just the heads of the older teachers who were nodding.

"Maybe I should rephrase the question: in each of these incidents, who has THE problem?"

"Well, the kids have a…, well, the problem… don't they?" suggested Kate.

"I reckon we have the problem," suggested Judy, the older teacher who was sitting opposite.

"Well, we are responsible, but the kids have the problem. We're responsible for making sure they mature in the long term, and making sure no one gets hurt right now."

"Doesn't that mean we have a problem, especially when we don't seem to succeed? I don't think the kids think they have a problem at all!" challenged Judy.

Kate, with the squabble just before leaving school still fresh if not raw in her mind, had been happy in justifying her approach. Now it was under challenge again, and as she felt a little resentful that her sense of satisfaction had been threatened, she wasn't quite sure as to whether she should argue or try to understand. But, she reminded herself, she was not so insecure as to need to have all the answers – deep down she knew she was frustrated, and wanted to try something else, and yes, this was an experienced teacher talking. The fight response died down as she decided to listen while a couple of other teachers tried to argue that the kids had the problem. When the discussion turned to trying to understand why the kids wanted to fight, Nick broke in again:

"Maybe Judy has a point? What if in each case, you the teacher has the problem here and the kids don't have any? Then, if that is so, and you want to solve YOUR problem, knowing why or what the kids are fighting about is only a distraction. Consider this proposition: the kids chose to fight or not to bother listening; that's what they wanted to do and that's not a problem to them. And, if this is so, why you have a problem is not a question as to why the kids are fighting. Rather, you 'own' these problems because you have taken responsibility."

Stunned silence. Then after what Nick had said, Kate couldn't help challenging with "That's upside down and unfair! It is our job to be responsible; we'd get sacked if we let kids do what they wanted to. We have a duty of care! We have to make them stop when they misbehave, and we have to make sure they learn, do their work!" She could feel herself getting flushed in the face as she thought about how unfair all this was, how often she had heard parents criticizing teachers. A couple of other teachers clearly felt likewise, expressing their frustrations in no uncertain terms.

"OK" said Nick, "Listen carefully to what you are saying. 'We must make them stop doing bad things and make them do what is good for them'. That suggests you are responsible for their behaviour."

"But I am, we are" said Kate.

"Well, if that is so, you are in an impossible situation, because at the end of the day, you can't make anyone stop doing anything they want to without being controlling, you being there, you standing over them. What happens when you are not there?"

"But as Kate said, our job means we are responsible- and we have to make sure we are there watching the kids all the time, on yard duty for example" came a somewhat frustrated voice from the other side of the group.

"Well," said Nick "how about discussing this in pairs or groups of three" and he wrote on the whiteboard:

KIDS BEHAVIOUR AND MISBEHAVIOUR
THINK?

1. WHAT = THE PROBLEM(S)?	2. WHO HAS EFFECTIVE CONTROL?
3. WHO IS RESPONSIBLE?	4. WHO IS HAPPY?
5. WHO IS STRESSED?	6. WHO OWNS THE PROBLEM(S)?

While teachers were discussing Nick went out to the storeroom and came back with a white vinyl basketball and two somewhat smaller balls and put them on the table.

"OK, what have you decided about the questions?"

The teachers generally agreed that the kids needed to be in control, taught self-control, and if a child was uncontrollable, then they had to be taken out of the school because in the end they were responsible for what went on. When kids misbehaved, they were unhappy, teachers stressed, and everyone had a problem. As teachers were reporting their discussions and without commenting, Nick then wrote on each of the small balls with black whiteboard marker: 'Behaviour.'

"Now let's make the behaviour more concrete." Nick then asked Judy and Kate to come forward. "Let's pretend these two are kids in my classroom. These balls represent? – yes, their behaviour." Nick went on as he gave them a ball each:

"Who has effective control of those balls?"

"The kids."

Nick went over to Kate's balls and drew ☺ and the word 'good' next to the word 'behaviour' on her ball. Everyone agreed that everyone was happy, no one stressed, and there wasn't a problem with that behaviour.

Nick then put the word 'mis-' in front of 'behaviour' on the other ball that Judy was holding, and drew ☹. As if on cue, Judy mischievously started bouncing the ball and running around with it, knocking over a coffee mug in the process. Grinning, Nick asked her to stop, but she ignored him. He jokingly threatened her with cleaning up the coffee cups after everyone had gone home.

"There's a dishwasher there anyhow, and that's simple to load," was the sassy reply as she continued bouncing the ball. Nick went over to take the ball from Judy, but she ducked away laughingly: "You're not allowed to touch me – remember, I'm a girl!"

Over noise of the bouncing ball Nick continued: "So much for power! So much for any effective control! But who is responsible here if something goes wrong? Clearly a case for stress, and what an invidious situation when we know from Organisational Psychology that the best way to get really stressed in a job is the senior-managers-dream/middle-managers-nightmare: to have responsibility for things over which you have little or no effective control. In the end I can't effectively control the ball, or Judy for that matter. Judy's happy, well sort of, but I am not!"

"How do we stop Judy? Do we have anything beside the threat or imposition of greater punishment? In the past this had been inflicting the physical pain of corporal punishment, and today we still torture no less but by inflicting psychological pain of some sort, including deprivation. Call it what you will, its punishment by which I hope I can cause Judy sufficient pain for it to give her a problem bigger than the one the *mis*behaviour is giving her, and I have an emotional pay-off in the resolution of my frustration, annoyance and perhaps even anger."

"Now, because I was a teacher, I have learnt to very cleverly rationalize: I tell myself that I am much nobler than that; it was really all about suppressing the misbehaviour so I could help her understand and take control cognitively: self-control. There might be a couple of problems with that though. Firstly, behaviourists will tell us that especially for extroverts like Judy, reward is many times, at least ten times, more effective than punishment. So, Judy just has to get satisfaction every once in a while, by getting away with the *mis*behaviour for her to be powerfully conditioned to continue next time. Then, if she has some sort of attentional problem, she won't be very aware of consequences past the immediate gratification, and unlikely to exercise cognitive control until it is too late. And if you are really angry, she is more likely to be left confused in dealing with your anger and feeling put down, and not hearing the content or think clearly about what you are 'lecturing' her on. In fact, she is unlikely to like you enough or feel you like *her* enough to be receptive to any of your advice."

"In the end, while you might get your way for the moment, it won't endure, but even worse, such a power approach doesn't lead to a happy classroom either." Nick had learnt much of this as part of Thomas Gordon's Teacher and Parent Effectiveness Training, and in his postgraduate studies has enjoyed finding the research evidence that underpinned it.

In the ensuing discussion, some of the teachers didn't agree that this was a power approach. Whether it was or wasn't, they all agreed that it was what any seasoned teacher had to do to maintain discipline and discharge their duty of care. It worked for most kids, but not for the real behavioural problems. They turned to Nick, challenging him as to what workable alternatives he had to offer.

"Let's have a look at what's going on here in this group, with Judy bouncing her ball". Nick added the groups' responses to the whiteboard:

KIDS BEHAVIOUR AND MISBEHAVIOUR

1. *WHAT = THE PROBLEM(S)?*   2. *WHO HAS EFFECTIVE CONTROL?*
    Judy's behaviour   Judy: i.e., student

3. *WHO IS RESPONSIBLE?*
Nick, ie ultimately the Teacher,
students should take responsibility, but with misbehaviour they don't.
We can't make them if they don't want to.

4. *WHO IS HAPPY?*
Judy who the student, well, sort of,
Except if Nick wins on the dishwasher,

5. *WHO IS STRESSED?*
Nick, ie teacher(s)
Kate and other kids

6. *WHO OWNS THE PROBLEM(S)?*
('that is who has a problem with the behaviour?')
While Judy's behaviour "is" a problem to the teachers & everyone,
Judy's only problem = the dishwasher

So, everyone else has a problem!
I am a fool if I take responsibility for what I have no effective control over. Extra problem!

Nick stood back and challenged: "OK, I want to challenge Judy's misbehaviour as being our problem!"

Some teachers wanted to object, but Nick went on: "Who has ownership of the misbehaviour? I haven't got hold of that ball but I do have a problem, so where is the problem?" He walked over and fetched the basketball, and coming back to the group wrote on it 'Problem.'

"Interesting isn't it, we have been so preoccupied, so fixated on the misbehaviour, distracted by that ball, the little ball Judy is bouncing, that we completely missed, left out, the REAL problem – the big problem, teacher stress by having responsibility for what we have no effective control over, and of course annoyance in having the peace interrupted by a kid with ADHD, a label which suggests the kid has no control either. Here is MY PROBLEM – I am holding it now. It is mine. And it's fair and square between Judy and me. I don't want it. In the end, it is the only thing I have effective control over. What can I do?"

"Get another job!" came a voice from the far side.

"Yea, that's one way of dealing with it. But if we don't want to run away, maybe we can deal with things constructively and effectively if we can understand some things that give us a handle. Notice where the ball is." said Nick, as he asked Kate to stand away from Judy so that the three were at the points of a triangle, with Nick holding the ball in between himself and Judy. "It is blocking my relationship with Judy, and while it has come about by Judy's misbehaviour, it is clearly mine. It is my problem! That means I can do something about it, and resigning isn't the only way!"

MANAGEMENT VERSUS LEADERSHIP: RELATIONSHIP KEYS TO
POSITIVE CLASSROOM CULTURE

He went over to the whiteboard and amended it:

1. *WHAT = THE PROBLEM(S)?*
   stress from Judy's behaviour

Nick went on with everyone's undivided attention: "Notice what I just said. 'It is blocking my relationship with Judy.' Herein lies a challenge about the sort of classroom culture I want. It's either a matter of control (power/authoritarian = extrinsic management and compliance), or it's a matter of relationship (democracy & intrinsic control and motivation). While there is a third possibility: do nothing, (permissiveness and anarchy), if I want positive harmonious culture and not a power dominated one, the research supports people like Thomas Gordon (Effectiveness Training), Rudolph Dreikurs (Social Discipline and Democratic Teaching Models) and Carl Rogers (Person-Centred Psychology), who all suggest that effective strategies must focus on the quality of relationship, not control. In practical terms, this simply means that if I am to operate strategically, I have to get that basketball out from between Judy and myself."

There was silence as everyone tried to come to grips with what Nick was saying, and he took the opportunity to draw four columns on the whiteboard:

Culture →	Authoritarian, top down	Democratic, equality	Permissive, indulgent?
Type of leadership →	Manager	Consultative leader	anarchist

"Here is the challenge," said Nick. "It is one of management versus leadership. Who here likes to be managed, or do you respond better to being led? A controlled classroom climate is one in which students' behaviour is a responsibility to be managed by the teacher. A positive classroom climate is one where individuals are led into taking responsibility for their own behaviour and learning. Positive relationships motivate independence and a sense of responsibility for self-management in any organisation. These are well established principles in organisational psychology.

I like a quote from Trish Jacobson (2002) writing on effective leadership in the *Canadian Manager*:

Management maintains a focus on
- *Planning and organizing;*
- *Controlling and problem solving;*
- *Focusing on outcomes.*

Leadership maintains a focus on:
- *Creating a vision and developing strategies;*
- *Engaging, motivating and inspiring people;*
- *Building trust and having courage; and*
- *Creating action.*

"Well, that's all very fair, nice and sounds logical, in fact ideological, and it might work with adults, but I have been around for quite a while, and as a teacher with a lot of experience of kids, and I like kids, I don't really think that kids can live up to that; they simply haven't got the self-control or the maturity."

Nick smiled. One teacher had spoken quietly, but with conviction.

"I'm just going to digress. I want you each to think of something you might have done or would hate to have done, that you would find very embarrassing. Just take 30 seconds."

There were some interesting murmurs and smiles around the group.

"Now, think of someone you know who would be the last person in the world you would want to talk about it with. Just take another 30 seconds."

"Okay," said Nick as he picked up a whiteboard marker and moved over to the whiteboard. "I'm not going to ask any of you to tell me what you thought about, who you brought to mind. Rather, tell me the sort of characteristics that person exhibits."

Very quickly the following list appeared on the whiteboard as teachers called out.

PERSON A

Judging   Talks at you   Factual   Directive   Judgemental   Preachy   Cold
Doesn't understand   Tells you what you should be doing   Gives lots of advice
Is impatient   Isn't really interested   Is analytical   Controlling   Severe
Proper   Lacks kindness   Doesn't like animals (giggles)   Critical of others
Insensitive   Gossip   Controlling   Has all the answers

"Now I'd like you to just take 30 seconds and bring to mind the person you probably most like to talk to if you've done something really embarrassing, or there was something really troubling you." The list on the board grew quickly:

PERSON B

Listens Empathic Understanding Principled Caring Forgiving Accepting
Knows what is right but doesn't tell you what to do
Non-judgemental Wise
Informed Considerate Gentle Has a mind of his/her own Ethical
Accepts/understands how I am feeling Doesn't gossip Fun loving Sense
of humour

"Finally, I'd like you to bring to mind a third person you know: a person you might often catch up with, you might even know quite well, someone who doesn't seem to ever mind what anyone else does, but is nonetheless also a person you would be unlikely to want to confide in or seek an opinion from.

After thirty seconds of reflection, the adjectives flowed quickly:

PERSON C

Calm Even temperament Agreeable Self-preoccupied Accommodating Quiet
Not easily flustered Unfussed Uncaring Unconcerned Irresponsible A-social
Dreamy Follower Disconnected Unthinking Adaptable

" Now, if I was to give these lists to the kids in your class and rate you against each of these words on a 10 point scale, how do you think you would come out? How about people in your family, or your own ratings of yourself?" There were smiles all round the group.

"Which sort of person would you prefer as your teacher?" As Nick paused, there were further knowing smiles around the group.

"In your school days, which teachers would you have wanted most to muck up on? Which teacher, if they ask for your help, would you most want to cooperate with? Which teacher would it be hardest to be nasty to?"

"Are you saying that we simply have to be namby-pamby, all nice and sweet with the kids and everything will be right? That takes a lot of work, and we simply haven't got the time for it," said Jeff.

"No and yes" said Nick "No: it's not simply a matter of being nice and permissive, but rather being the sort of person who, while having standards, the kids also find it easy to trust; where there is a trusting relationship that has been built over time. And Yes, that takes time, yet in the long term saves time. Now the aim here is not to produce kids who are just going to do what they are told because they feel beholden to you. That would still be being a dictator, albeit a nice one."

Questions for reflection

Which of persons A, B or C best describes who you are most of the time?

Which would you prefer to be, and why?

How are you going to make a commitment to change?

Nick returned to the columns and asked the group where each of the three might fit best, and then went on to ask them to nominate the characteristic role, emphasis, control structure, and who carried responsibility for each. After some discussion the board looked like this:

Culture →	Autocratic	democratic	permissive
Type of leadership	authoritarian	facilitative	anarchic
Style of leader	Person A: Boss/superior	Person B: confidante/ collegial	Person C: unremarkable
Role	Manager	Leader	unengaged
Leadership Emphasis	Management	Cooperation	chaos
Control structure	Topdown control	Mutual responsibility	none
Responsibility	Topdown	shared	Defacto leaders

"Where do you fit most easily?" asked Nick as the group reflected.

"Well I reckon the autocratic is the most efficient" came Jeff's immediate response. "I'd like to be democratic but we don't have the time. And I would prefer to call what you name 'autocratic' 'authoritative.' It might be OK with your own family or peer group, but with a bunch of kids from all sorts of backgrounds, some of them quite dysfunctional, well as they say, the buck stops with me. A little bit of authoritarianism never hurt anyone, especially if it was done in a caring way. "

"Yes" came another voice, "how can you make democracy work among kids who lack impulse control?"

"Seems to me how you teach has a lot to do with your personality and how you were taught and how you were brought up," continued Jeff.

"Well, there are a lot of challenges," acknowledged Nick. "These three differences have been noted for some time, and Rudolph Dreikurs (see reprint Dinkmeyer

& Dreikurs, 2000) some three or four decades ago showed how you succeed democratically with the most challenging students, so let's look at the disruptive Judy from a democratic view."

Nick asked the other two members of the group to stand where they had stood before, holding the "problem" ball between himself and Judy.

"Remember, this is my problem, and if I have in the past developed a good relationship with Judy, I should be able to get her to come over to my side and deal with it." Nick turned to Judy.

"Imagine that I'm a person you quite like, a person who's listened to you in the past. This is a very important factor here: I'm a person you quite like, a person who's listened to you in the past. Now, Judy, I have a problem, and I was wondering whether you might be able to help me?"

Nick clearly held Judy's attention as she looked positively at him.

"Would you mind coming around here and looking at this ball with me? And Kate, could you also come around here and help me deal with this ball?"

The three now all stood together opposite the one ball. Nick turned to the group.

"Can you see that I'm not blaming anyone, but it's quite possible that with the next few words Judy will feel some guilt, and may even want to exonerate herself. That would in fact be a really good sign, indicating that she knows she is doing something that she really shouldn't, and this is really a form of self-censorship. I'm going to try and avoid in any way implying any blame by avoiding the word 'you' as much as possible, that is, I'm going to try to avoid any you-messages. You-messages always blame and put people on the defensive and distract them from constructive cooperation, in fact distract them from factually looking at what they need to focus on. So, instead, I need to demonstrate ownership by stating everything as much as possible as my problem, and that is best achieved by stating things in terms of 'I' – that's what is called and I-message. So, can you help me frame what I should say to Judy? And Judy, listen to what they suggest and go and stand where you think that would make you feel you should be."

"I need that behaviour to stop" came the first suggestion. Judy started moving away from Nick.

"Yes," said one of the other teachers "that might be efficient, but you've simply left out the word you – it's really saying 'I need your behaviour to stop, because you are annoying me', implying blame. How about first making a positive statement about what she is doing?"

Nick turned to Judy. "Judy, I see that you are having a lot of fun bouncing and playing with that ball, and I know that school can be a bit boring for someone with so much energy, in fact, I'd love nothing more than for us all to join in a game with you."

While Kate moved away a little, Judy, continuing to bounce the ball as vigorously as ever, nevertheless slowly but surely had moved a little back toward Nick.

"I have a problem right now that I can't solve without your help. We all need to get some other stuff done right now, and we can't do that without your willing involvement."

35

JUDGING

"I can see how that would work if you and Judy had good mutual respect, but not if she was suspicious of you" reflected Michael. "So what do you do with someone who is a ratbag?"

"Isn't considering any student a ratbag a little, well harsh, maybe just a little judgmental? I find that once I have used such a negative label for a person, it simply doesn't leave me anywhere to go other than writing them off," suggested a quietly spoken Yvette who had been silent until then.

"Well, it's just a manner of speaking. No need for political correctness here, surely. We all care about the kids and I am sure you all know what I mean," came Michael's somewhat defensive reply.

"I agree, we see no harm and mean no harm in such shorthand" Nick said. "But language is powerful, insidious, it can be a Trojan horse that brings with it unchallenged implicit assumptions. Names can really hurt you despite the old saying."

"I think Yvette brought out the points I wanted to make very nicely. Firstly, getting cooperation will only work in an environment where you have established mutual respect, and secondly, the best way to prevent that is not to use labels that imply bad motivations. The latter is something that comes so naturally to me and even though I have done training programs, I can still slip up! It's all around us. We model it as we grow up. It is so common place that we don't recognise its destructive power. But stop and think about it. Think of someone you recently gossiped about or felt angry at, where you felt they were doing what they did for the wrong reasons. Once we judge a person as having bad motives, we have nowhere to go with that person, and they have no comeback. We have blown the relationship. Now let's analyze it a bit further in terms of the two sorts of people we thought about earlier: this is being the first type of person. It destroys trust and community."

"What's the alternative? Can I suggest the challenge of choosing the type of person you are going to be, by refusing to be judgmental, carefully watching your language and self talk, and as the father of effective counselling, Carl Rogers demonstrated that utilizing the power of showing everyone unconditional positive regard. We know from research in counselling and therapy, as well as in teaching, that the most significant factor in effectiveness is the relationship between the helper and helpee."

"Don't you think that's a bit idealistic, if not naïve?" asked Jeff. "I don't think we have a choice. Some people really do have bad motives, and if you don't recognise them, you will get hurt. You have to be at least a bit street-smart in this life if you are going to get on, if you are not going to be taken for a fool." Looking around the group Nick could see that some of the others clearly agreed.

"Mmm, well," said Nick, "are you suggesting that in reality, to survive in the world, you have to be more like the person 1 than person 2?"

"Well yes," said Jeff. "You can only have good relationships with a small number of people; there aren't many people who are really thoughtful and trustworthy and in the end non-selfish."

"Okay" said Nick, "each of you recall the first two people you brought to mind." On the whiteboard he wrote the questions:

Which one:		
do you like more?	do you respect more?	has more friends?
has better relationships?	is happier?	is healthier?
is wealthier?	feels fulfilled?	is taken for a fool?
is astute?	is less stressed?	

After some discussion, all agreed that the second person they thought of won on each of the points except for wealthier, being taken for a fool and astuteness: Wealth being a mixed bag and the other two both were generally pretty much equal.

"It is interesting" continued Nick "that the second person you thought of can be astute without being judgmental. And that is where we have to leave it this week. Next week we will look at specific techniques as to how we can get those who have given us a problem to help us *solve* the problem without being authoritarian. This means getting the ball out from between us. In the meantime, you have quite a bit to reflect on back at your schools. And please remember that changing the culture takes time and skill."

Kate's notes centred around three pictures of three people: in the first, two were holding small balls and one very large ball in the middle separating them; a second with all lined up together and the big ball in front of them; with the third the big ball was soaring up about to go through a couple of goal posts. Below that she had written *"One team, one goal: Shared responsibility through mutual respect."*

Questions for reflection

Are there any professional and personal development goals you might like to consider setting?

How are you going to achieve them?

BUILDING INDEPENDENCE AND WELLBEING INTO A POSITIVE SCHOOL CULTURE

OVERVIEW AND KEY CONSTRUCTS

- Effectiveness: an integrated approach.
- Ownership: developing self-control and responsibility.
- Recognising judgemental negative thinking.
- Replacing Automatic Negative Thoughts (ANTs) with Automatic Positive Thoughts (APTs).
- Active and Reflective Listening.
- I-Messages and You-Messages.
- Application of an effective integrated approach.
- Building a constructive repertoire, defeating old destructive habits.
- Dealing with severe adjustment problems.
- Positive psychology.
- Drilling down to a common goal: wellbeing and happiness.
- Student empowerment and problem ownership.
- Unconditional positive regard: the positive relationship of understanding.
- Locus of Control and Self efficacy.

Meet the Cast

Main Characters:

Kate – Teacher
Nick – School Psychologist

Minor Characters:

Karl – a "naughty" boy at Kate's school
Mayur – a student at Kate's school
Robert – Junior teacher at Kate's school
Megan – Kate's artistic sister
Jason – Secondary student with severe behaviour problems

EFFECTIVENESS: AN INTEGRATED APPROACH

It was Saturday afternoon. Kate had enjoyed the peace of working in the garden, and come in for a cup of tea. As you do when you relax during repetitive physical work, she had found herself cogitating, churning over and over the previous afternoon's details. She recalled the role-play and pondered on how what she had learnt yesterday might change the way she would deal with Louise and Jenny's after school squabbling incident. She decided to get out her notes as she sipped her hot tea. She needed to reinforce her new understanding, preferably before she was back at school on Monday if she was to retain or use the learning. She wanted to recapture the sense of hope she had felt when she wrote "one team, one goal," and the yearning for a greater sense of cooperation with the students in her class had resurfaced while she was enjoying the tranquillity of her garden.

Questions for reflection

Mindfulness can help you be more effective in creating a positive school environment:

Have you noticed that the best times for reflection are often when you are doing menial things like gardening, walking, and house-keeping ?

Do you take advantage of quiet reflection? or keep yourself from thinking by bombarding yourself with entertainment / information from your phone or portable music player?

She recalled how she had started to understand that she needed to focus on the big ball and not be distracted by little ones. Identifying problem ownership gave a different perspective. If she framed the incident in terms of identifying her problem, well, it was that she felt responsible for stopping the squabbling. And how had she tried to do that? Of course! By going straight to the content, the little balls, trying to be reasonable, reassuring, joining the argument.

Clearly she needed to add what Nick had suggested she should avoid. And, yes, now she thought about it, somehow she felt sucked in and, well, sort of found herself saying things she really didn't mean or know about or had a right to say. In fact, she thought, Louise was sort of right: Jenny's drawing wasn't very attractive, but then, she couldn't really speak for Nan, in fact she didn't even know Nan. By playing the small balls she had joined in their game! The kids were oblivious to her big ball. She had never even realised it was there! But now....

"OK, so if I don't need to consider the small balls, I could solve my problem by exercising my authority: just tell them 'you must stop this squabbling'" Kate's thinking continued reflectively ...that, and a little moral lecture maybe would be a quick and economical answer in the short term. Ah, but what was the bit in the session about an authoritarian approach? And the word 'you' suggests that it would really be sending a you-message. And then, it still felt like she was taking responsibility for stopping them, clearly evident by the potential frustration that would follow if they were to ignore her: in which case she would need to ramp up the power.

The big ball was still firmly between her and the girls. No team playing in that scenario! How to make it a team game? How then could she get the kids on side to solve her problem: how to get them to want to stop squabbling, by sharing in the responsibility? It dawned on her: the girls were oblivious to the big ball! She had to tell them about the big ball and get them on side to help her with it! How could she do that without blaming, she wondered, as she remembered Judy moving away in the workshop?

There was Nick's emphasis on needing to build a climate of mutual respect. Did the students see her as someone they would want to trust, a confidante? Someone who was not judgemental? But they were young. Was it too much to expect? She shuddered as to how they might rate her if she gave them the list Nick had written up. How hard we work at only allowing people to tell us what we want to hear, she thought. The phone rang. It was her sister Megan. Would she like to come to dinner? Kate's first impulse was to wonder whether her sister was ringing her out of duty, or pity for her being on her own.

"Hey, stop mind reading – what's our problem?" came an unexpected voice from deep in her subconscious. As she thought it through, she felt a sudden release from judgement, and found herself surprised by the warmth in her own voice as she found herself saying, "That would be great Megan – thanks for thinking of me."

She put the phone down, and needed to understand what had just happened. She was normally in control. She knew her normal automatic response was "No, I'm fine, I have already got something organised for tonight." It was based on trying to second guess the reason Megan would invite her over: a sense of obligation or feeling sorry for her living alone! All of a sudden she realised that even if that were so, that was Megan's problem. Any feeling of Kate being judged was her own problem. She would enjoy not having to cook for herself tonight, and indeed, enjoy one of Megan's creations: she had a knack of putting ingredients together in interesting and balanced ways.

On her way out to Megan's, Kate grabbed some silver beet from the garden, and a few lemons, and yes, some broad beans. When she arrived at Megan's, she discovered Megan pottering in her own kitchen. She pulled out some nibbles and offered Kate a pre-dinner beer. As they started chatting, Kate's two young nieces came over to say a polite "hi" to their aunt, and on seeing the nuts, made a grab for them. Not a murmur from Megan. Kate felt her sense of irritation and responsibility rising. "Hey, stop mind reading – what's our problem?" *An internal debate had begun.*

"These kids should have better manners. They are being spoilt. They won't eat their dinner."

"Is that our problem?"

"Well no."

"Then what's our problem?"

"Those kids aren't really here because of me – they just know a visitor brings out nice nibbles. I'm not even sure they like me."

The inner dialogue continued: "Automatic negative thoughts: ANTs. Remember the recent program on Cognitive Therapy?" Kate recalled the useful material she had found on the internet on ANTS after seeing the program. "No use knowing if it doesn't translate into doing" fleeted through her mind, but it was the immediacy here that distracted her from following this through: Kate sensed herself blushing as she realised that her nieces had little reason to like their stern, negative thinking, judgemental school-teacher aunt. After all, when had she taken any *real* interest in them recently?

"Aren't we mind-reading again? ANTs undermine good relationships, let alone your own wellbeing, and we have a problem we have to solve." Kate was suddenly aware of having been distracted, deep in thought, and Megan saying "Had a pretty full-on week? Where were you just now?" And for the first time since they were children, Kate accepted her sister's care and concern for what it was, and, for the first time in a long while, *felt* her sister's natural warmth.

"Oh," Kate replied, "yes, it has been getting harder at school, but we had a PD on Friday, and it has given me lots to think about. Couldn't really get it out of my head while I was gardening today."

Megan was a good listener, so over the next hour Kate's thinking from the last 24 hours came together and it all poured out. She had been reflecting on their father, loving but autocratic, distant, well-meaning, but controlling, judging and preaching, and how she felt she was just like him. How she always felt responsible, prided herself in being responsible, making herself be responsible for everyone else, and how jealously she had grudgingly admitted to herself that despite having the same father, Megan was the quintessential understanding, non-judgemental, accepting yet principled listener who seemed to have unconditional positive regard for people, irrespective of what they did. Now in tears, and so caught up in the torrent that was pouring forth that she wasn't aware her sister had her arm around her, Kate asked Megan if she thought she could ever change: could she ever stop the ANTs?

Megan didn't answer immediately. She didn't affirm, gainsay or make light of anything Kate had said. She had just been there, listening intensely though. And then Megan quietly asked, "Remember the one about how many psychologists it takes to change a light bulb?"

"Yes," Kate answered, "one, but the light bulb needs to be willing." Kate had often wondered what people meant when they said they had experienced an epiphany – now she realised she had just had one!

The next morning, a bright sunny Sunday, Kate woke up feeling emotionally exhausted but unusually optimistic, though a little wary as well. She decided to spend another day in the garden, but by 11am she wanted to go inside and dig up the material from a workshop she had been to last year on 'building rapport and trust in teaching'. Understanding 'problem ownership' had unlocked the issue that so far had stopped it from making sense. She had understood reflective listening, active listening as they called it, as a means of establishing trust so that students would like you enough to do what you told them to in dealing with their problems. But now she saw that suddenly very differently.

She could use reflective listening to help individuals become aware, just as Megan had in allowing her to reflect last night, without saying very much at all – just being there, accepting her unconditionally, and then superbly handed over problem ownership with the light bulb analogy. She had never thought she could see her sister as a role model, but with still a little twang of reserve, she acknowledged that maybe she could learn from her, and most certainly from a couple of other people who had come to mind in the exercise, people who one could turn to and who would also most likely be comfortable confiding in others too. They were all really good listeners. Kate looked through the lists she had copied down on Friday, and considered again which ones others would most likely tick about her. How much, she thought, were they the ones people would also have marked about her father. She wrestled with the thought of fighting her genes. She was Kate – and how could she ever change? She recognised the ANT pushing into her thoughts – consciously replacing it with a positive thought: she *was* going to change that lifelong destructive habit by cultivating positives – APTs!

"Well," she determined "at least this bulb is going to do all it can to change." During the afternoon Kate first spent half an hour searching the internet for material on dealing with automatic negative thoughts, finding plenty that she bookmarked. Then she pulled out the material from some recent workshops, working her way through a number of exercises on constructing active listening statements, as well as the 'road block' exercise.

That afternoon flew as Kate searched the internet for further useful material: she was surprised to find a lot on active and reflective listening, road blocks to communication and problem ownership. Kate also found YouTube material from the Gordon Training International based on Dr Thomas Gordon's *Effectiveness Training* to be particularly helpful.

APPLICATION OF AN EFFECTIVE INTEGRATED APPROACH

On Monday morning, as if part of some conspiracy, the first children to arrive at school were Louise and Jenny. It seemed so long since Friday, but not for the twins.

Within minutes, Kate's attention was distracted from writing up on the board by the girls bickering. Here was an opportunity for Kate to put her understanding and practice into action. Jenny was already in tears.

"You're feeling a little unhappy, aren't you Jenny?"

"Yes," replied Jenny, "Louise says the other kids only like me because I am her sister and they want to play with her because she is really good at basketball and I am not."

Kate felt instinctively she wanted to resolve the issue with a quick reprimand to Louise. The scenario had played itself out many times between the twins; just different content each time. Instead of feeling this was her problem, however, with the insights and practice of the weekend behind her, she recognised that the only person here with a problem was Jenny, and her role as teacher was to help her learn to deal with the problem, and if possible get Louise on side as well.

She had to get her head around this fast. It wasn't automatic – not yet. As she thought about it though, the problem seemed to be that Jenny allowed her sister to put her down. This understanding helped Kate avoid what she might otherwise have done: join in the power struggle by telling Louise off for being nasty. It was after all a set up by the twins, with Louise watching on carefully. Previous actions had simply served to maintain the scenario time after time. "Active listening," thought Kate. "Active listening no matter what. No judgement. No taking sides. And, every ANT is an opportunity for a APT." She brought to mind how she had seen both Megan and one of her other role models handle such a situation.

"And you are really upset with your sister saying that?"

"Yes" replied Jenny, glaring at Louise as if waiting for Kate to turn and reprimand her. But Kate just kept her gentle focus on Jenny, and nodded, acknowledging: "That must feel horrible."

"She is always being nasty like that to me" continued Jenny, pushing to get Louise into trouble. But Kate kept her focus on Jenny and what Jenny was feeling and then planned to move on from her feelings to her underlying beliefs.

"I understand how horrible it feels when a sister says things we don't like, but do you think she is right?"

"No, she isn't!" Suddenly Jenny's tears started giving way to more assertiveness, and her shoulders straightened up. Kate felt she had been able to get onside with Jenny against her problem instead of it being handballed to her. Now that Jenny felt a little understood, she was also changing gear, from unconditional acceptance reflecting the emotional to moving to the rational/cognitive, ready to challenge her misbeliefs.

"So, if you don't believe your sister, why do you accept what she says?"

"Because Mummy says she shouldn't say those things!"

Kate wanted to ask Jenny why she thought her sister might want to say hurtful things, but past experience had taught her that that simply resulted in blamefully attributing bad motives, and the need to address these by engaging with Louise.

Instead she now realised she needed to get Jenny to focus on taking responsibility for what she could control herself.

"It really feels horrible when your sister says things like that, and your mummy is right. So, how do you think we can help your sister stop doing that?" Besides Jenny's sudden look of indignation, Kate also caught a look of surprise on Louise's face.

"But," protested Jenny "it's her fault, and, ... and, well, she just shouldn't be allowed to say things like that and make me feel unhappy."

Kate recognised that Jenny was not getting what she was accustomed to, winning the power play, and was turning up the volume by playing the victim role hard. There were also issues of an external locus of control: she was blaming Louise for her own emotional state. If Kate was not careful, Jenny would become very upset, in which case Kate would need to change gears back to listening, but that would take time. While in terms of seriousness this was a relatively low level game, it was laying a pattern for far more damaging and serious habits in later life. Here was an opportunity to squelch the emerging cycle. This was not a time for explaining what was going on and telling Jenny to take responsibility for her own feelings, but it was an opportunity 'by doing' to give her some skills to jump out of the victim-perpetrator frame.

"And you don't like being unhappy, do you? It feels terrible."

Feeling she was gaining leverage, and possibly feeling understood, Jenny responded with "Yes"

"And you would really like to feel happier. You can't make your sister stop, especially when there is no one else there, but you know, you could ask your sister if she would like to help you be happier"

"I could, but I know she doesn't want me to be happy."

"Well, we don't know that for certain: so why don't we ask her."

Kate was finding that keeping her eye on the problem, keeping Jenny's ball in focus at all times, was helping her focus clearly on remaining 'on the ball.' Most surprising was the good feeling that came with her newfound freedom of not needing to solve a problem of her own. Identifying the real ball in the room, and having revised reflective listening and changing gears gave her somewhere to go without needing to resort to power.

"Jenny, there are lots of times I see you playing together where you look like you are enjoying what you are doing. Is that right? Can you tell me of times when you enjoy doing things with Louise and you are happy?"

"Yes" Jenny responded slowly. "When we made breakfast in bed for mummy and daddy last week, and when she watched our favourite show with me last night and when we talked about the new bicycles we are getting in the car on the way to school this morning ...."

"OK then," said Kate turning for the first time to Louise who was standing there curiously watching the whole procedure, "please tell Louise how you enjoy doing these things together with her and ask if they make her happy too." Jenny asked

Louise, and Louise said they were fun for her too. "Now ask if Louise likes you to be happy."

Louise answered, "yes."

Kate continued, "And now ask her if she would like to help you with a problem of being unhappy when she tells you that you are no good at something."

Before Jenny could say that, Louise had turned to Kate and said: "But sometimes Jenny is just stupid!"

Kate refused to engage directly with Louise, but taking this as an indication that she was not ready to come on side to help with Jenny's problem, she decided to teach Jenny to be assertive by sending an I-Message. Based on what Kate had learned from a workshop on positive psychology and Albert Ellis's ubiquitous ten irrational beliefs (various iterations readily available on the internet), Kate went on to a discussion with Jenny about what 'water off a ducks back' meant, and that everyone did silly things sometimes; that people quite liked others who did silly things as we all had things we are good at and things we are not so good at; that whether they might be true or not, and things people say might not be nice, in the end it is we who can decide to ignore them or take them personally. She then asked Jenny if she had friends of her own, to which she replied she did. Kate asked Louise to tell her three things she thought others liked her for and Louise was able to answer quite quickly.

Having dealt with the cognitive work underlying Jenny's ANTs, and having established a positive base for APTs, all the while conscious that Louise was watching every fine detail, Kate now asked Jenny to pretend she, Kate, was Louise and to laugh at her no matter how she felt when Kate repeated what Louise had said. This worked beautifully, Jenny not only laughing, but giggling as well.

Next Kate asked Jenny to simply repeat after her, and saying it to Louise, 'Everyone enjoys being stupid sometimes. Not everyone likes everyone, and my real friends like me 'cos I am me, and if they only like me 'cos I am your sister, they aren't real friends'. Next time you say things I don't like, I am going to laugh at you. It's going to be water off a ducks back."

Though Louise was clearly somewhat embarrassed, both girls then laughed. Kate sent them off to play. It hadn't been easy, but Kate felt she had empowered Jenny to recognise, own, and deal with her own problem. She was rather proud of how she had managed to stay out of being the superpower who comes in to adjudicate a conflict. This had taken just over fifteen minutes instead of three, but in the long term Kate knew it was time well spent. It didn't take much coaching subsequently to help her out of it.

Kate knew that basically, Jenny and Louise had been no great problem. While her success had burned itself as an ideal into her mind, she wasn't so sure how it would work with more difficult cases. In a few of these, lacking confidence and finding old habits die hard, she found herself in the fray of the day, with no time to think, resorting to her well-honed previous behaviour management techniques.

Questions for reflection

Analyse Kate's approach in terms of:

- where you see various particular balls being at various stages
- the use of various techniques such as active listening.

How might such new patterns be developed and maintained in the future?

BUILDING A CONSTRUCTIVE REPERTOIRE, DEFEATING OLD DESTRUCTIVE HABITS

While Kate had made a mental shift and experienced some success, old routines and habits are often deeply engrained. Kate was still always rushing; an over inflated sense of responsibility someone had once suggested. Well, she thought in defence of her relapse, if only there were more responsible people in this world.... all very well to have these reflective practices, but where does anyone find the time? Kate had tried to keep a log of types of interactions with students, as Nick had asked, but she knew she had done that far too irregularly, in fits and starts. None the less, from time to time her success with Louise and Jenny had the effect of getting Kate to reflect somewhat on what she was doing. This happened most clearly when one day, feeling less rushed, she had paused to think before acting. She had taken time to talk with Karl, a boy who could be quite wilfully naughty and distractible, and connected with him about writing a story about his trail-bike riding accident.

She had been very happy with how engaged he had become as she practiced her active listening, focussing much of the conversation on reflecting on what Karl had felt. But the glow she felt crashed when, within seconds of returning to his group, he started to poke and wrestle the boy next to him. She felt betrayed and angry, with a feeling that he had taken advantage of her. She was about to take control, and though she would not admit it, exact some revenge, by sending him over to the time-out corner when she drew breath just long enough to hear rising from her subconscious: "Hey, stop mind reading – what's our problem?"

The thought rang so clearly that it stopped her in her tracks. It served as an anchor: "Where is that confounded ball?" she asked herself. And then, she saw it, clearly. "It's my problem! No it isn't! Yes it is – identify and don't take your eye off the ball!

It's our feelings that are the problem. And I am justifying myself, pumping myself up by mind reading, attributing malevolent motivations and cunning wilfulness to a boy who probably just has some attentional and self-management issues, and when all is said and done, is pretty straightforward." Karl was still letting off steam in his scrum and it struck her that rather than spitting in her face, this might be little more than some sort of displacement behaviour, some compensation for the discomfort of the unusual experience of feeling accepted by his teacher.

"Whatever," she thought, at the very least she understood this much: his misbehaviour was her problem, not his, and the ball was dangerously in between them, threatening the good work of the affirming discussion they had more recently enjoyed. Kate needed to think fast: how to manoeuvre him to get him on side so that they could together tackle her problem? No, manoeuvre implied manipulation, and that was covert power. Rats! She needed to get his free and willing cooperation she had been given to understand. She was trying to recall. But how? Maybe share it with an I-Message. But how? It didn't come to her automatically.

She started walking over to Karl. He wasn't looking in her direction. He had his mate in a headlock. And as she walked she was aware that she wanted Karl's help in solving her problem, but she might not get it. Karl released his mate as he suddenly became aware of Kate standing next to him, and his friend was about to return Karl's favour when he too stopped in his tracks on realising that Kate was standing next to them. They both looked sheepish, expecting a reprimand. But even to Kate's surprise it never came. She addressed both of them:

"I have a problem that I was hoping you two could help me with." In her mind's eye she saw them coming around from the other side of the ball as they both nodded their consent. Kate was desperately looking to make I-messages, thinking about starting sentences with 'I', excluding the word 'you', and avoiding covert 'you-messages'. Keeping an eye on the ball seemed to be helping. Her problem had now resolved into getting Karl working rather than stopping the misbehaviour and hoping that somehow that would motivate him to apply himself to his work.

"I really enjoyed hearing about your trial-bike riding Karl, I learned heaps and think I understand a little about how you enjoy it even though you might sometimes hurt yourself as you do in the accident." At this point in time she thought to draw in Karl's friend as an accomplice.

"Do you do any trial-bike riding, Mayur?" she asked, in the process winning some time in which to frame a question that would get them to help with solving her problem without focussing on it in a negative way.

"No, but I am saving up, and Dad said if I got a much better report from school I might be able to get one at Christmas."

"OK," she said, "Well, I am really looking forward to Karl writing up his accident as a good story so we could share it with others, including how the helmet probably saved him from serious injury. What can we do to get this under way quickly, and what do you think you might be able to help, Mayur?"

To Kate's surprise, Mayur suggested that they could turn the writing into a project and that he could find pictures of trail-bikes and helmets, and even some facts about helmets while Karl could write up his story, and it could take centre place.

As Kate left the pair focussed on their project, she realised that she had not spoken a single word about their misbehaviour, and even though she was aware that Mayur's father was applying some extrinsic motivation, she had not bought into that, though she had been sorely tempted to use it for some leverage. She reflected on how the resolution involved encouraging *intrinsic* motivation. This surely must be what they meant by a positive classroom culture, she thought.

A few weeks later though, when he was in the area, Nick dropped by her school following up on the PD. Here was her opportunity to share some of her successes, but also to challenge him about its limits. Secretly, she was looking forward to stumping the "know-all." How applicable was the positive classroom for kids who really had problems, who had definable psychological conditions, like those who suffered from 'mental' problems such as ADHD, ASD spectrum, and learning problems?

Questions for reflection

How applicable do you think these methods are with individuals who really have major social adjustment problems?

Can you imagine how you might need to adapt these somewhat?

DEALING WITH SEVERE ADJUSTMENT PROBLEMS

Nick listened quietly. "Well," he said, "you know all kids are much the same, and the same things apply. We are so quick to blame others for our problems. There are a number of key constructs that we can learn from positive psychology. Primarily, we all want to be happy, which really means we all want to have a sense of wellbeing. Everything we do is motivated by a subconscious intent to improve things, make us happy or happier. It's just that many of us don't understand what makes us happy; we blame others and get into power struggles, we don't grasp the opportunities when we have them."

"How come you seem to have all the answers, Nick?" asked Kate, wanting to hide her attraction. "But didn't Freud help us and the advertising industry to understand that motivation is ultimately all about sex?" she challenged in semi-jest.

"Ah, such a good point" responded Nick, "I don't have all the answers – what I have learned is not my opinion, but based on good research in positive psychology which sees even sex as a means to an end, not an end itself."

"A means to a few ends – like having kids as well as pleasure?" suggested Kate.

"Well, ultimately those other ends could be considered as no more than things on the way to what we believe will make us happy. We have kids because we expect them to make us happy."

"Or maybe it is out of a sense of duty" challenged Kate.

"And what do you think someone fulfilling their duty does for them?

"I get your point. So you think we are all fundamentally hedonists then?"

"Not quite. I understand hedonism as the self-interested pursuit of pleasure in the belief that pleasure is the ultimate good. Positive psychology can attract a cult following from many who erroneously think that it is the pursuit of pleasure for its own sake. In reality it is about evidence-based ways of knowing, that is, utilising the science of achieving and a healthy pervasive sense of wellbeing that we identify as happiness. Working at achieving a healthy psychological state of wellbeing is no different to working at being healthy physically by eating and exercising well. A healthy mental and physical state of wellbeing is good not only for us, but everyone around us. It is an effective antidote to the epidemic of depression that is enveloping the developed world."

"So, what does positive psychology have to offer the classroom teacher?" asked Kate

"The key issues from an educational and developmental point of view that make for happiness involve identity, growing up being comfortable with ourselves. As Victor Frankl put it, knowing who we are, where we are going, and who is going with us. Can you see how that would involve self-acceptance, self-determination and self-control? That's where positive psychology comes in, by showing the importance of an internal sense of locus of control and an independent sense of self-efficacy as essential for happiness. These are keys in creating a positive classroom culture."

As Kate wrote the terms down, Nick suggested that probably the most convenient way for her to learn more was to look them up on the Web. Kate returned to her earlier challenge. "That's all very well Nick, but again how about the really damaged kids who suffer from things like problems such as ADHD, ASD spectrum disorders or learning difficulties? This theory is all well and good for kids who are pretty well OK, but surely we need to be practical in managing and controlling these others, and this is where behavioural methods are best?"

"I don't agree. Remember I started off by saying that everyone needs to be happy? The other differences don't matter nearly as much as we think when we invest in the positive approach. Differences are too often used as an excuse to exclude, and people who have a need to control, all too often hijack behavioural measures as a tool to be used to that end. People who want to shape the world in their own image scare me. They don't understand the limits of their understanding or the potential evil that can come even from power that is benevolently motivated. A positive approach that avoids the power game also avoids the victim-perpetrator paradigm and makes for a happier society.

"Enough of the theory. I understand you want to see it working at an applied practical level, so I'll give you an example. I have just come from one of the secondary colleges down the road. The principal just sent me a thirteen year old who they are at their wits end with in that he is a real behaviour problem. I had it laid on me that I was their last hope or he was out. They had tried everything, I was told, including a tightly managed behaviour modification program.

"Now, that's not a nice ball to get passed, a bone everyone has had a chew at, and I wasn't about to accept the impossible. I have limited understanding, but some basic principles I am convinced of because I see them work, and there is also good research evidence. This is a kid who has honed his skills to defeat teachers over seven years of school. He knows exactly how to play the power game. So, I said to the principal, 'Well, you know, I can't make him do anything any more than you can; I can't fix him, and even if I could force him to change I wouldn't, because for me that's ethically unacceptable.'"

"The light bulb bit" butted in Kate with a grin.

"Yes, exactly. If I was to have any chance of effecting change, it would be because the lad chose to make that change himself. So, I told the principal that I was happy to speak with him, if he would like me to, but I could promise nothing, to which the principal said that at least he would be able to put the consultation on the paperwork as evidence that he had done all he could.

"Jason had swaggered into the counselling room. Arms folded, it was a situation with which he was long acquainted. I knew he had convinced himself that everyone else had a problem, and he felt in charge. Meantime, I felt free of any problem ownership. Simply, if I could, here was a lad who was in denial about having a problem that was ruining his life. No 'musts' or 'should be' for me here; only the simple desire that if I could ,get him to recognise and then own his problem, I could perhaps help him to deal with it for his sake. Jason was now my client. Until he came to realise that he had a problem and that he had sole control, he would be fighting everyone else to make sure he was their problem. It's all a blame-game around power, and the moment I entered into the power game, I would lose.

"But isn't the school your client? It is they who have called you in, asking for help. They have the problem don't they?" asked Kate.

"Well, the way I see it is that he is their client too. But they are enmeshed in a power struggle because they have taken responsibility for his behaviour rather than leaving it with him, and as soon as I join in with that I would be setting myself up for a certain failure certificate along with everyone else. I am sure that there are a lot of very clever people trying to help this fellow over the years, in the process training him to stay in charge. My only hope is to come from a completely different angle, admitting that I am completely powerless in regard to his misbehaviour. While I would like the school to be happy with Jason, that would be a by-product."

"So, did you last more than 5 minutes?" Kate was curious now.

Nick went on to say that he'd simply accepted the fact that Jason had come into the room as an indication that not all was lost. Jason had slouched down in the chair, trying to look nonchalant, yet arms defiantly folded: all too familiar to Nick. Nick gave Kate a quick rundown of what had actually happened, pointing out how positive principles could win through:

"Well Jason, I'm Nick. I guess you don't really want to be here?"

"Its awright. Beats class" came the short answer. At least he's talking thought Nick. Nick's goal was simply to get alongside Jason, and he knew that would be neither easy nor easily sustainable. To do that he would have to show unconditional positive regard and stay out of any power challenges, and in any way own Jason's behaviour problems as Nick's.

"Well, I don't really want to be here either," said Nick, by implication not accepting Nick's denial about not wanting to be there.

"So why are you here then?" asked Jason.

"Same reason as you – I have to be here, to earn a living, and the school has asked me to see you because they think you have some problems."

"Well, I ain't got no problems. The school's got the problems: they want me and some of my mates to do all this dumb stuff that we don't want to, and they can't make us do nuffin anyhow,.... and you can't neither" challenged Jason. Nick was amazed at how clearly right up front Jason was able to sum up the entire power conflict.

"Bang on, Jason. I can't make you do anything, and nor would I if I had any real power, because at best I could only get you to do what I wanted while I was holding a gun to your head so to speak."

Jason rather liked the idea of a gun. But he was suspicious. "So, what you here for? To write another one of them reports?"

"No. I told you, I wouldn't be here if they weren't paying me to be here. I hate writing reports. They don't do anything for anyone except the filing clerks. No, when Mr B the principal asked me to see you, I told him I didn't think I could do anything, but he wanted me to talk with you anyhow, so I thought 'OK, I'll listen to Jason's story'."

"I ain't got no story to tell."

"So you are telling me that Mr B simply wants me to see someone for no reason at all?"

"Well, how would I know – I'm not Mr B, am I?"

At this point Nick was feeling Jason's resistance was palpable. There was a determined hostility in Jason's voice and demeanour. He just wasn't managing to get alongside Jason in any way. In fact the opposite: Jason wasn't even admitting now that the school might have a problem. He could either push on ignoring the denial and build on the earlier admission, or changing track and rapport build around some common interest outside school ("I'm not sure why, but instinctively I felt the better option was to change track", Nick reported to the group).

"What did you do on the weekend?" Nick went on.

"Nuffin much"

"Just as boring as school?"

"We went shooting." Nick understood this to be another power statement and wondered whether he was meant to look shocked or impressed by an under age, uncontrollable boy with a gun. But he stayed away from any matters of concern and went straight to opening a window for sharing feelings.

"What sort of gun do you use?" Nick asked Jason, looking for an opportunity to share his interest in the sport.

"A Ruger – 10/22 longarm."

"I use a Remington 700 BDL with iron sights" said Nick grasping the opportunity, and it was immediately obvious that he had made a connection.

Nick continued to relate to Kate what had happened over the next ten to fifteen minutes: they enjoyed sharing about guns and shooting vermin, Nick learned a lot about Jason. Jason went shooting with his father and uncle on his uncle's farm. He held a junior shooter's permit. He prided himself on knowing a lot about gun safety. He was such a good shot his father had said he could make the Olympics. Nick asked Jason if he knew what might be required for getting into a team. Jason knew little about target shooting clubs.

Nick asked Jason what going shooting did for him. He replied that he really liked being outside. Nick asked him what being outside in the night air did for him. Jason said it made him feel free. And then Nick asked him the chain question again: what did feeling free do for him. It made him feel happy.

Chain questions are a useful technique for drilling down to real purpose: the questioner keeps inserting the respondent's reply into the same question until ultimately there is nowhere to go. This endpoint often usefully clarifies the ultimate goal.

	Questions for reflection
	1. Take something you do, perhaps something you would like NOT have to do… Ask "What does x do for you?" and chain onto each answer
	2. Try it today: Run the exercise with a friend or student
	3. Practice it weekly to get really familiar with it as a skill

"So Jason, ultimately you want to feel happy?" Nick had asked somewhat rhetorically. A little more guardedly, Jason agreed. Nonetheless, it was time to return to the matters concerning school, thought Nick sensing strength in their talking together.

"What do you want to do for a living after you leave school?" asked Nick.

"Professional Roo Shooter" was the immediate reply.

"What would 'Roo shooting do for you?" asked Nick starting the chain question again. Jason followed through: he would make money doing what he enjoyed; making money would allow him to do more of what he wanted which included living in the bush. Living in the bush with his own house would make him happy. Yes, he wanted to be happy for no reason other than that he liked being happy.

Nick felt that he demonstrated enough unconditional positive regard in sharing to establish enough trust to tackle Jason's problem without the defences rising to block.

"Meantime we have a few years of school to deal with. School doesn't make you happy does it?"

"No." Jason was visibly tightening up. Nick was determined not to enter the fray. He wanted to grasp the momentum to get Jason to deal with the ball before he had a chance to go into denial.

"I wonder what we can do to stop school being such an unhappy place for you?" Nick was careful not to blame either school or Jason, but to encourage a sense of problem recognition and ownership.

Jason sat there for a moment, and then tried to deflect the question with: "School sucks. Teachers are nerds." Jason wasn't accepting the ball.

Nick went with it but without compromising himself: "Yes, I know, but you will never be able to change the school. Pretend you are Mr B. What would you do with Jason?" he asked while watching the body language keenly. Nick pointed out to Kate he often used this role-reversal play as an acid test of the quality of that trust that had been built. Jason didn't disappoint, though to Nick's surprise, Jason also demonstrated the authoritarian paradigm he understood all too well: the problem person turned vigilante.

"I'd chuck him out, or detention every day 'til he picked himself up and got to work."

" So, there are things Jason does that the school doesn't like?" suggested Nick trying to get Jason to acknowledge a problem, which Jason did, but at the same time justifying himself.

"Yeah, but that's because they deserve it. They are such nerds they just don't get it."

Keeping it in the third person, Nick asked Jason: "So, what does mucking around do for Jason?"

"It gets him into trouble."

"… and what does getting into trouble do for him?"

"It makes him angry and get even."

"Does being angry make for Jason being happy?"

"Nu."

"But you want to be happy, and school makes you unhappy because of what they do when you muck around? How would it feel if you felt the teachers respected you? If you really want to be happy at school, do you know you could have the teacher's respect?"

Jason sat there silently, thinking, and after a moment: "Nu, never."

"Well, I reckon that together we could work this through and make it happen" challenged Nick, "but it's your choice."

"Yeah, but how?" asked Jason. Now Nick knew that Jason was acknowledging the problem and entertaining some ownership, the initial rays of hope that come from a glimmer of self-efficacy and empowerment. Time was running out and he had to plan for the next session. Nick knew he would lose ground between now and then, but there was hope.

"Well, if you are happy to talk next week when I am back – we can talk it through more, and we can even role play some of your teachers and explore alternatives for you. And, we can make sure you don't get into such trouble as to stop you getting a full gun licence when you get to that age."

By the level of attention the last comment drew, Nick commented to Kate, he knew that he had a chance to move Jason from the recalcitrant victim role caught up in a power paradigm to one that takes responsibility for how others treat him by taking responsibility for his own behaviour.

But for now, cutting short his time with Kate, Nick needed to be off, to a school down the road.

Questions for reflection

The narrative about Jason is based on a real case.

Where and how were you challenged by the case study of Jason?

Did keeping your eye on the ball help you understand what Nick was doing?

Jason reflects disengagement typically found in a rural culture. Can you think of an exemplar of inner-city street-wise disengagement, and a potential scenario for facilitating self-efficacy?

Two months later when Nick next dropped by, Kate wanted to hear the next episode! Nick had found out that Jason experienced reading difficulties. He was able to report how seeing Jason's behaviours as maladaptation rather than wilful, and keeping his eye on the ball enabled him to make progress so that the school was no longer talking of exclusion, but in fact was providing extra support, notwithstanding some tensions from time to time with some of the more authoritarian inclined teachers.

UNDERSTANDING BELIEFS AND PROFESSIONAL PRACTICES

OVERVIEW AND KEY CONSTRUCTS

- Beliefs about teaching
- Reflective teaching: from theory to practise

Meet the Cast

Main Characters:

Tracy – Teacher
Tom – Student with ongoing behavioural issues.

Beliefs have a significant impact on how you teach and what you teach. Think about a child, Tom, who you might strongly believe should not be in your classroom. The reasons for your beliefs may largely be based on how Tom behaves, and perhaps also on your ability to deal with his behaviour and its effects on others. The report from Tom's past teacher states that "Tom is often non-compliant, shows little interest in what is being taught, and on some occasions has shown his aggression by picking fights with others and tearing up his workbook". Reflecting on my experience when I first started teaching, I would have been terrified by the thought of having such a child in my classroom. I must confess here that I am presuming that a majority of teachers prefer not to have such children in their classrooms. The presumption is based largely on my personal experience, observing teachers in regular and special schools, teaching pre-service teachers at universities, and a large body of research that indicates that teachers are least receptive to teaching students who display "disruptive behaviours". This is not to deny that there are many teachers who are challenged by those students who display disruptive behaviours on some occasions, and that such teachers work hard to make students like Tom feel welcome in their classrooms. Unfortunately, however, research shows that generally speaking, the majority of teachers are reluctant to have such students in their classrooms (Daniels & Cole, 2010).

Now, my question is: does it matter if teachers believe that having students with disruptive behaviours in their classrooms is undesirable or unworkable? How would it affect the way they teach? I will ask you a series of questions and would like you

Questions for reflection

Would you like Tom to be in your class? Why? Explain the reasons to your Principal.

If your reasons are accepted, what would be the likely consequences for Tom?

to reflect on your teaching practices. You will find it useful to closely examine your responses and determine if there is a need for you to change the way you teach, or if you are already doing most of the things that a reflective and effective teacher would do.

We know there is plenty of research that indicates that teachers who would prefer not to have students like Tom in their classroom but are then required to teach such a child are not able to do him justice (Daniels & Cole, 2010; Rogers, 2000). One such teacher is Tracy. She pays attention to Tom when he misbehaves rather than when he behaves appropriately. She provides few opportunities that allow Tom to show his potentials. For example, she asks him questions less frequently compared to other students in the class, and she also provides fewer examples to explain difficult concepts when Tom dares ask something about which he is not certain. As a result, Tom starts behaving or continues to behave consistent with the way Tracy believes is typical of him. In other words, her beliefs influence the way she interacts with Tom.

There is evidence available that our beliefs are self-generating, simply based on conclusions drawn from our selected observations (Argyris, 1990). Research also shows that we tend to choose data that matches our views and understanding of the world and we tend to ignore data that does not fit into the schema we have created, to help us understand the way things should work in every day life. We use such selective observations to draw conclusions, adopt beliefs, and then act according to these beliefs. Tracy believes something is wrong with Tom and/or with his family, so she continues to treat Tom as someone with a problem. She believes she can do very little to change her teaching practices to accommodate Tom's individual needs. She prefers to refute research which shows that a change in her teaching style might improve Tom's classroom behaviour, since such research is not congruent with her beliefs about Tom's behaviour.

If we understand that beliefs can and do influence our teaching, the next question concerns how we identify and change our beliefs. We are presuming that a teacher such as Tracy has recognized that her beliefs are not conducive to effective learning for Tom and she needs to do something about it. There are many ways that a teacher's beliefs can be changed. One important means of achieving this concerns reflective teaching.

WHAT IS REFLECTIVE TEACHING?

According to Dewey (1933), an early leading authority on reflective teaching, there are two kinds of teachers. In one category, there are teachers who believe in routine action and impulse, where tradition and authority is essentially enacted in their professional behaviour. These teachers continue to teach in a routine way, "as long as everyday life continues without major interruptions" (Grant & Zeichner, 1984, p. 104). They continue to find this the most efficient and effective means to teach and to solve problems that are largely defined or perceived as having been created by others. Such teachers look forward to finishing their day so that they can go home to the things that they *like* doing. In the other category there are the reflective teachers, educationists who frequently ask questions about their teaching and are able to be self-critical. We have seen examples of this type of teacher described in the previous chapters in this book. They look back at their teaching, review and evaluate, reflecting on what happened and seeking to understand why it happened. They frequently change the way they teach to accommodate the needs of their students. They look forward to the challenges at school and the opportunities in teaching students and even in learning from them.

Long ago, Dewey (1933: p. 9) defined reflection as "active, persistent, and careful consideration of any belief or supposed form of knowledge in the light of the grounds that support it and the further conclusions to which it tends." It may be useful to think about this definition and how it applies to your teaching situation. This explanation suggests that if you are a reflective teacher, you will continuously question your beliefs and practices. In a practical way, when you come across a new theory relevant to your teaching, you will first closely examine the theory, and then test it out before fully incorporating it into your teaching, or alternatively dismissing it.

Reflection thus forms an important part of problem solving (see, Loughran, 2002). The act of teaching effectively requires teachers to be able to see the problem from different perspectives. We need to frame and reframe the problem; this allows us to identify actions that we would not have taken if we had not continued to look at the working context from just one perspective. It is easy to recommend that educators should learn to view educational problems from different perspectives; in reality it is very hard for educators to do that, unless constantly reviewing their own practices. This is by no means an easy task, yet an essential element if trying to teach individuals who do not fit a preconceived 'norm'. , In the previous example, Tracy believes Tom remains disengaged in the class because he is lazy and disinterested in learning. If she takes this perspective to solve the problem and continues to see the problem as Tom's, she is less likely to try new ways to engage Tom in her class. If Tracy sees the value of looking at the problem from another perspective, she may find that Tom is disengaged because he does not find the material interesting and thus lacks motivation to learn. This different perspective shifts the focus of the problem to other aspects, and now includes considering problem ownership that must involve the teacher. She is now more likely to look for solutions that will require new ways of teaching that potentially, ensures that Tom can become more motivated to learn.

This not only will help Tom to be engaged but it will also lead to a more adaptable learning environment that also benefits other students. An ability to look at the classroom context from different perspectives is a fundamental attribute of a reflective teacher, a person who is willing to create a positive learning environment for all students. Another important aspect of being a reflective teacher is that you may need to accept that something you believe to be right could indeed be wrong (Larrivee, 2000). These ideas are well summarized by (Boody, 2008), p. 506) who reports that a truly reflective teacher, "is not only willing to talk, but to listen deeply, to be open and relatively non-defensive, to consider the possibility that what she was doing/thinking was wrong or at least inadequate and then to act, even at the cost of personal pain and change". This is not an easy but important option as part of good and effective professional teaching practice.

Moreover, reflection should not just be seen as a new technical skill that must be learned in order to be considered a better teacher. Reflection should also enable a moral and personal response to what happens in the classroom, creating a culture in the classroom based on mutual respect, unconditional positive regard, and understanding. Without such a value system, a large number of students may experience a sense of isolation and lack of connectedness in school, since the teacher focus remains on fixing the student, with very little time given to changing the classroom culture where our students need to feel a sense of belonging.

In order to be truly reflective, Dewey had suggested teachers need to develop three important attributes: 'openmindedness', a sense of 'responsibility' and what he called 'wholeheartedness'... Interestingly, research on open mindedness shows that most people see themselves as far more open minded than others see them. Open mindedness is an active mean to examine the many facets of one issue. A teacher who is open-minded is likely to be receptive to new information, and others' viewpoints (Garmon, 2005). Accordingly, teachers who lack open mindedness risk either rejecting new information or interpreting it in ways that will be consistent with their current views. The second attribute identified by Dewey is responsibility. These teachers are deliberate in taking responsibility for their actions and consequences. On occasions a teacher's actions may be deemed troublesome or unacceptable by the school. But being a reflective and responsible teacher, she will take responsibility for heractions and be prepared to deal with the consequences. The third characteristic, Dewey suggested that wholeheartedness acts as a fusion that like glue helps to

Questions for reflection

1. Do you consider yourself to be openminded?

2. Is being a responsible teacher something you can be without becoming overly responsible for changing others?

3. Does Dewey's concept of wholehearted bother you? Why?

bind a teacher's commitment to the two characteristics of open–mindedness and responsibility. Implications of these three attributes are discussed in greater detail shortly.

WHY DEVELOP REFLECTIVE TEACHING?

The use of reflective teaching allows teachers to make a significant shift from their existing belief system. A teacher who reflects on her teaching frequently, is more ready to realize when a change in her teaching is necessary and when such change would improve the learning of all students, and increase her own satisfaction with teaching. It becomes an intrinsically driven need to change practices, not initiated by an outsider but realized and initiated by the teacher herself. It is therefore likely to result in longer lasting change. Many teachers, including Tracy, make judgments about their teaching based on what they had personally experienced during their years of schooling (Christensen, 2004). It is therefore possible that during these years of modelling, Tracy also had frequently observed her teachers controlling disruptive behaviour by sending a student like Tom, to the Principal's office and accepted this as an acceptable strategy for dealing with such students. When asked to include a student like Tom in their classroom, teachers will naturally look to evidence from their past experiences in support of either segregating or using alternate strategies to manage the inappropriate student behaviours. Use of reflective practice may allow Tracy to re-think her past experiences of teaching and learning and to re-conceptualize her notions of effective teaching practice (Christensen, 2004).

It is widely accepted that the incidence of behaviour problems in schools is increasing and it remains one of the most stressful issues for teachers (Daniels & Cole, 2010). Schools are generally responding by ensuring that teachers in their schools undertake professional development in how to effectively address problem behaviors. This seems like a right step in addressing the issue. However, there is one problem with it. Teachers may learn technical skills such as managing student behaviour, creating engaging classrooms and keeping students on task. However if the skills do not mesh with the personal beliefs of the teachers, it is less likely that skills learnt during professional development will be sustained. According to Larrivee, (2000, p. 294):

> [When] teachers become reflective practitioners, they move beyond a knowledge base of discrete skills to a stage where they integrate and modify skills to fit specific contexts, and eventually, to a point where the skills are internalized enabling them to invent new strategies.

Questions for reflection

Reflect on a professional development activity you undertook recently. Do you think it merely provided technical information or was it closely tied with your belief system? Are you likely to use what you learned during the PD program? Why or why not?

To sum up: the use of reflective practices allows teachers to both challenge then change existing beliefs, which is likely to result in their using better teaching practices congruent with their beliefs. The change in beliefs thus promotes practices that sustain a more positive culture in classrooms. Once a teacher has reached this stage, then teaching new skills becomes much easier.

HOW CAN YOU BECOME A REFLECTIVE TEACHER?

As hinted at in the previous chapter, you cannot become a reflective teacher unless you want to be one. There is no one way that a teacher becomes reflective. You will find it useful to think about a reflective teacher as one who believes (attitude, with the Heart) that being a reflective teacher is good for her teaching, cognitively knows about reflective teaching (with the Head) and who practices (with the Hand) being reflective. This is reminiscent of Pirsig's account of motorbike appreciation, utility and maintenance (p. 9, ch. 1). For the teacher on the 'educational road trip' there are ways and means of better enjoying the experience, better doing the work and staying safe and sound. In other words, you need to have Head, Heart and Hands (3Hs) of a reflective teacher to teach like a reflective teacher.

One cannot become a complete reflective teacher unless you possess and/or use all three Hs. The first H (i.e., Head) of reflective teaching requires you to know what reflective teaching *is* and why should you be a reflective teacher. This information is already covered in the first part of the chapter. The second H (Heart) of the reflective teaching requires that you have the necessary attributes (open mindedness, responsibility and wholeheartedness) to teach effectively. These three attributes are like three pillars that form the foundation for becoming a reflective teacher. If any of the three 'pillars' in this construction are weak, the foundation will not be able to sustain the use of reflective teaching practices. These 'pillars" are explained more fully in the next section.

Openmindedness

This is an attribute that demonstrates you are open to new ideas and constructive criticism about the way you teach. It also means that you believe that teaching in your class could be improved and such an improvement will make the classroom a much better place for all students including Tom and a satisfying experience for you. To quote Grant and Zeichner (p. 104):

> Being a reflective teacher means that you keep an open mind about the content, methods, and procedures used in your classroom. You constantly re-evaluate their worth in relation to students currently enrolled and to the circumstances. You not only ask why things are the way they are, but also, how they can be made better.

The reflective teacher understands that one of the reasons Tom is misbehaving, could be because he has not yet found a teacher who understands his version of the story. The reflective teacher also understands that giving voice to students, listening to them and asking them questions about her teaching, could lead to better solutions to many problems the class is facing. The teacher is also willing to learn from other teachers, parents, and students in her class and also students in other classes.

Responsibility

Teaching is a moral and ethical responsibility (Grant & Zeichner, 1984). The decisions we make about what we teach, how we teach and what resources we use to teach will have a profound impact on what students learn and what they do in the school and outside the school. For example, if Tracy believes in promoting racial harmony in the class, she will mix students of diverse racial background to work in small groups. The group will understand that their success is interdependent on how well they perform as a group, rather than individually within the group. She will also use resources (e.g., text books), that show the value of appreciating diverse racial backgrounds. On the other hand, if she does not believe in racial harmony, she will pay little attention to how students are grouped and may choose resources that fail to promote the idea of racial harmony (e,g., choosing a book where children of only one race are represented).

Another way of being morally and ethically responsible lies with the way a teacher interacts with students. For example, she would find time to play with Tom in the playground, would ask questions and provide positive feedback to him, would provide leadership opportunities to him (e.g., taking attendance roll, library monitor). These interactions are strong signals to everyone in the class that Tracy values Tom for the things he can do well. It must be emphasized here that it is not easy for most teachers to find good qualities in a student who has often been identified as "a problem behaviour child". A child's disruptive behaviour often clouds all current actions and future reactions of a teacher. The child is only seen as "the behaviour problems child" rather than a child with lots of abilities and strengths.

Wholeheartedness

Wholeheartedness is the 'glue' that binds open-mindedness and responsibility. A teacher who lacks this attribute is someone who says one thing and does another thing. Think of a teacher, who often says "I believe in social equity, that all students should be given an equal chance to succeed and we should never use punishment". However, you know this is the teacher with whom Tom spent his last year. Tom's report does not indicate that he was given any chances to succeed. On the contrary, his

Questions for reflection

Is your teaching philosophy congruent with your teaching practice? ,This might be a good time to write your own teaching philosophy. Most importantly, include students like Tom in your statement. Where do they fit? How do you see such students being taught? Why do you think they should be taught this way?

Then reflect on your teaching practices – are they consistent with what you wrote or believe in? If there's a mismatch between what you believe and what you do, then it is time for you to either re-write your teaching philosophy or change your teaching practices.

report states that he has been sent to principal's room many times for inappropriate behaviours. You also saw this teacher singling out Tom for an incident in the playground, for which he was not responsible. Another classical example of lack of wholeheartedness is when teachers say they love and enjoy teaching all children. What they really mean is not *all* kids but *some* kids who behave well or who are highly compliant (Grant & Zeichner, 1984).

It is possible that you are already doing many things that a reflective teacher would do. This section presents a more systematic way of how you can teach like a reflective teacher. We are aware that teachers have limited time and to teach like a reflective teacher could be seen as an added responsibility. But as Scheffler (1968: p. 11) put it:

> Justification for reflection is not ... simply a matter of minimal necessity. It is rather a matter of desirability, and a thing may be desirable, not because it is something that we could not do without, but because it transforms and enhances the quality of what we do and how we live.

For those of us who are used to teaching in traditional ways, becoming a reflective practitioner is going to be challenging. If you have decided to teach as a reflective teacher, be prepared that initially the journey may not be as smooth as you might be expecting, but it will be highly rewarding in the end. To practice as a reflective teacher and create a positive learning environment for all students, including Tom, you need to be reflective at two levels. Firstly, share your experiences in being reflective with others – question what you are doing to improve on past practices. Secondly, engage your students in evaluations of what they need, and how it might best be achieved.

Level One: Evaluating and Changing Self-Practices

Asking appropriate questions to evaluate what is happening in your class, is fundamental to the art and craft of reflective teaching. Teachers who never question their goals and the values that guide their work, the context in which they teach, or never examine their assumptions, do not do justice to their students or to themselves (Zeichner & Liston, 1996). Asking questions about your teaching practice will allow you to grow and become a better teacher. An encouraging thought: One indicator of whether you are an effective teacher would suggest that disruptive behaviours become minimal.

A model that may be helpful: SCREAM

If you need a structure to help in becoming a more effective teacher, you may find the following of use: it is but one way to help you conceptualize your teaching practice, particularly with younger students, or those who struggle to organize themselves or be self-motivated. An effective teacher is sometimes described as a *SCREAM* teacher (Mastropieri & Scruggs, 2010). Yes, a SCREAM teacher! SCREAM teaching is characterized by

Structure (establishing what will be taught, with clear objectives),

Clarity (use of examples to clarify difficult concepts),

Redundancy (targeted practice until all students have understood what needs to be mastered),

Enthusiasm (love teaching the subject and that is quite evident in the way you teach),

Appropriate rate (know the learning levels of your individual students and ensure that you do not rush through the topics nor spend too much time so that it becomes boring), and

Maximised Engagement (keep the whole class engaged by effective questioning and feedback, and by placing them in small co-operative groups).

The survey below may be useful: Self rate yourself on each of the items and then ask your students to rate you on each item. Compare results to see if there are any discrepancies. I highly recommend that you do this exercise so that your students are not identifiable by their responses. You can also use your peers to evaluate your teaching practice/style.

Read each question carefully – then circle a response that best describes the way your teacher/ Mr or Mrs X/ teaches.

Do you know each day what you will be learning?	Always Sometimes Never
Do you know at the beginning of a lesson what you will learn by the time the lesson is finished?	Always Sometimes Never
Does your teacher explain all the difficult ideas so that you understand the topic completely?	Always Sometimes Never
Does your teacher use examples to explain what is difficult?	Always Sometimes Never
Do you get enough opportunity to learn about what is difficult in class?	Always Sometimes Never
Does your teacher allow all students to practice when he/she has introduced a new topic, so that you understand it well?	Always Sometimes Never
Does your teacher enjoy teaching?	Always Sometimes Never
Does your teacher make learning fun?	Always Sometimes Never

Do you think your teacher looks forward to teaching your class when you return to school after holidays?	Always Sometimes Never
Do you think your teacher spends enough time on each topic in the class (neither too fast nor too slow)?	Always Sometimes Never
Does your teacher ask questions to understand the learning level of all students?	Always Sometimes Never
Do you feel comfortable asking questions about something you are not sure of?	Always Sometimes Never
Do all students get an opportunity to respond to the questions asked?	Always Sometimes Never
Do you get sufficient feedback on your work?	Always Sometimes Never
Do you get sufficient *positive* attention from your teacher?	Always Sometimes Never

Questions for reflection

Spend some time to self-rate yourself on the survey. Do you have many items where your rating is "never"? If yes, what do you plan to do about it? Do you think your students' responses will match your responses? How confident are you about it?

Self-evaluation, feedback from your peers and from students should provide you with some idea of what you need to do to make your teaching more effective. I recommend that you do such evaluation of your teaching at least twice in a year: at the end of the first teaching term (around 3 months after the beginning of academic year) and at the beginning of the last teaching term (around 3–4 months before the end of academic year). The first survey will tell you something about your teaching and what needs to be improved. You could use the survey information to change the way you teach. The second survey will tell you whether what you changed has made any difference to the way you are teaching now. If you feel confident, you can ask your students about how best you can improve one of the aspects where you scored poorly in the survey. You may be surprised with some of the ideas that may provide real improvements to your teaching. The process of evaluating your teaching practice may do two things: first, it is likely to make your classroom more engaging for all students and second, send a strong message to your students that you value their feedback.

Level Two: Using Evidence-Based Practices to Change the Classroom Culture

The survey provided above may assist you in determining if you are teaching well. While it is an important tool for creating a more conducive environment for all, you may face situations or incidents (e.g., Tom tearing up worksheets) that still occur despite you being a SCREAM teacher.

We suggest that reflective practice and evidence-based practice should be used simultaneously to improve your classroom culture and to deal with such incidents. Applying evidence-based practice (EBP) requires educators to be aware of the best available, current, valid, and relevant evidence, so that they translate that research into something meaningful for their classroom situation (Bannigan, & Moores, 2009). The aim of EBP is to help teachers to identify and then cease using ineffective practices, in preference for proven effective ones (McCuskey, 2004). Many educators continue to use practices entirely reliant upon custom and practice, simply using anecdotal or familiar old practices rather than using research evidence to guide their educational decisions.

When asked why they teach in one particular way, many educators respond by saying that they do it intuitively. One of the fundamental problems with being intuitive is that intuition is not always right and should not be the only guide for the practices of educators (Doust & Del Mar, 2004). Bannigan and Moores (2009) have described a useful model that integrates reflective practice and evidence-based practice. We believe use of this model enables educators to solve educational problems more effectively. The model consists of three stages: "What?" "So what?" and "Now what?" A description of these three stages is presented below.

STAGE 1: WHAT?

The process of reflective practice begins with a challenging or a disturbing event. It is an experience that leads educators to being unsettled, disquieted or angry. It requires educators to revisit the incident to make better sense of it. An example of such an event could be: an unexpected student reaction to a task (e.g., Tom tearing his worksheets), a comment from a parent that may challenge attitudes and beliefs, or an unsettling comment about your educational practice by one of your colleagues or your school principal. One of the fundamental tasks at this stage requires educators to describe the event as objectively as possible. This set of needs to be addressed in stage 1 relates directly to the management of problem ownership as described in Chapters 3 and 4. There is a danger that a teacher will only be concerned with her own perspective and feelings when analysing "what" happened. You need to be aware of such feelings and should avoid dwelling on emotional responses when describing the event. Ideally, it should be done when you have had sufficient time to allow emotions to settle, and that then you can hope to be more objective in describing the event. When an event is examined honestly it should not only identify how the situation has affected you but also reflect on how you may have contributed to the situation. Note this is focussed on what happened – asking why can only be considered after the details AND emotions have been considered or listened to.

STAGE 2: SO WHAT?

The second stage of the model suggests the teacher analyse the incident to understand *why* the incident happened, *what* she could have done differently, and what she has *learnt* from it. It is an important adjunct here to note that one believes such a critical analysis of the incident and a resultant change in teaching practice is possible, and, would enable her to be a better teacher in the future. This aspect of analysis involves reflection on the rationale for her actions. This is the most significant aspect of the reflective process. Why did the teacher decide to deal with the incident in one way rather than another? What relevant or potentially inappropriate source of information did she use in making the decision to act as she did? Unfortunately, some teachers make decisions based on knowledge derived solely from their past experience, without looking for alternate sources of knowledge of best practice. Boud and Walker (1998) describe this as "celebrating naïve experiences". Teachers should avoid being so self-directed that the basis of their decisions for action rests entirely on their own experiences.

Reflective teachers look beyond the immediate and search for knowledge that could explain what happens in their classrooms. They also look for proactive practices that might prevent such incidents and that also offer alternatives for dealing with them more effectively in the future. This essentially involves searching for evidence-based practices (EBP) – a corner stone in the construction of being a reflective teacher. Searching for new knowledge in relation to a particular incident is not always easy. This book provides some insights into current best practice, but we also know that knowledge evolves and what is best practice today may not be the best practice tomorrow. Publications of research in online format do provide alternative options to some extent, but access to a wide variety of educational journals is still a challenge. Schools and educational departments need to be encouraged to subscribe to the most widely known educational journals (e.g., *Intervention in Clinic and Schools*), to assist staff to keep up to date with the most recent knowledge.

Deciding to utilize new knowledge into teaching practices can be achieved in several ways: Sharing such knowledge with your colleagues allows you to clarify what you have understood about it; Ask a colleague to observe you using that new knowledge/practice, with honest feedback on both its application and how well it works. You can also attend professional development programs to learn how to apply the strategies you have read about, to gain additional confidence in making changes that might improve your teaching practice.

STAGE 3: NOW WHAT?

Once you have critically analysed the incident using an evidence-based practice framework, you need to know whether or not your practices are consistent with the best practices. A decision has to be made about your future actions. You may decide to continue past practices since they retain significant supportive evidence of their efficacy. Alternatively, you may decide to change the way you have previously dealt with a similar situation (like removing Tom from the room after tearing up his workbook, or alternatively listen to his frustrations, then find a way to fix his book), and, reflect with him about preventative strategies to address the incident before it occurs (e.g. Tom using a signal card asking for help when feeling frustrated).

In a majority of cases when dealing with problem behaviour, a change in existing teaching practice is both helpful and imperative, in response to such questions as: Is

Questions for reflection

You read about the three Hs of reflective teaching. Reflecting on these, do you think you have the head, heart and hands of a reflective teacher? Even if weak in any one of the three areas – how do you plan to make the foundation of reflective teaching stronger?

what I have been doing working?: Am I convinced that I should make a change in the way I teach? What changes are likely to make a difference? If you begin to make changes half heartedly, not convinced you should, it is unlikely that you will be able to sustain the new behaviour. Sometimes, maintaining a routine past practice is easier than trying an innovative idea. But an effective change in practice at this stage can occur if you realize that: 1. your current practice is not perfect, 2. research has shown better ways of dealing with the situation, and 3. that translating that research into practice may be tough but necessary for creating a positive learning environment for all the students in your classroom. And the bonus? a much celebrated personal satisfaction in you being more able to enjoy your chosen teaching profession.

POSITIVE LEARNING

Translating Research into Practice

OVERVIEW AND KEY CONSTRUCTS

- Evidence-based teaching
- Motivation and engagement
- Need to belong
- Choice theory in the classroom
- Resilience in the classroom
- Effective teaching strategies

Meet the Cast

Main Characters:

> Liam – parent of a student at odds with the school due to behavioural issues of his son.
> Mr. Fred – A smart principal.
> Cynthia – a sceptic teacher

Minor Characters:

> Tom – a student with behaviour problems
> Mr. Jones – teacher in Fred's school.

In this chapter we return to the teaching road trip and a narrative to explore a range of issues pertaining to the positive learning environment. One parent wanting to contribute to an engaging classroom is Liam, who has just arrived at the school. As he walks into the schoolyard, the serious lack of discipline is clearly a big issue. Students in the playground are using unacceptable language. He walks across the corridor only to hear Mr Jones, Grade 5 teacher, shouting for students to be quiet. But Liam is on his way to the principal's (Fred Stone) office, and he looks stressed. The reason he is here is because his son was suspended from the school for verbally abusing his teacher, Mr. Jones!

After brief but congenial introductions, the conversation speedily turns to the reason Liam is talking with Fred the principal: his son's behaviour. Initially, blame lingers in the air about who is responsible, but it is soon evident that Fred is solution focused, and very aware that this is not a matter of blame, but of people pulling together cooperatively. Fred is interested in finding out ways Liam can work with the school to improve his son's behaviour. Fred acknowledges that the school is going through a tough phase and he unapologetically asks Liam for his patience and support. He is clearly committed to building cooperation to make this school a better place for all. Fred has been head hunted and has been transferred to the school, as he has been successful in the past in transforming school cultures. The school's culture and standing in the community had recently tumbled because of significant discipline issues. Many parents have withdrawn their children and sent them to other schools.

While the names have been changed, the real school on which this story is based does exist and it actually lost over 50% of its students in less than 2 years. There are many more similar stories. With the school on the verge of closing, with a worsening reputation and an increasingly dysfunctional school climate, most members of staff were highly stressed. Fred realized that he had to look for resources outside the school to improve the situation. Experience had taught him that the whole school culture needed to change. School staff needed to be supported in regenerating a positive learning culture supported by constructive discipline.

Top down authoritarian control was not Fred's way. It would only last as long as the authority was there. And that was what had happened in this school: an 'authoritarian' principal followed by a 'laissez-faire' one who had previously been considered highly successful in a small specialist and highly affluent private school. Unfortunately, the current school had suffered a collapse in management and, as many members of the local community agreed, effective school leadership was missing. Fred believed that the only enduring way forward would be if the teachers and community gained a renewed sense of ownership and empowerment over the problems facing the school.

Fred was under no illusions as to the magnitude of the task. He ascertained that it would need substantial outside support if he were to truly engage his teachers and parents in reviewing and implementing effective change. Fred had been inspired by some of the research and by his mentors, when he had completed his master's degree in Education a few years ago, so he contacted the Faculty of Education at his Alma Mater, to find out what support, particularly by way of professional development, they could provide.

The rest of this chapter tells the story of this change, involving professional and organizational development. It offers an account of how support and research evidence can facilitate change in a struggling school such as Fred's, to create a more engaging, inclusive school environment. Also, without the conviction and commitment of the principal, and wholehearted support from the department of education, change is unlikely to happen. Fred remained aware that some teachers were entrenched in their approaches to teaching and anticipated resistance for what he hoped to achieve. Fred was certain he needed to get alongside staff, earning their confidence and trust by showing them positive unconditional regard and acceptance, meeting them in the 'here and now' of day-to-day work.

Many members of staff were very stressed, and to some degree most had established a range of self-defence behaviours against being blamed and abused. Clearly outside support would be necessary if teachers were to be helped to face the need for change. Outsiders coming in would need to gain teachers acceptance and approval before any application of research-based interventions discussed in this chapter would have any acceptance, no matter how well validated. Furthermore, these principles are not only relevant for dysfunctional schools; understanding them allows schools that do not have any significant problems with behaviour, to strengthen environments so that discipline will not be an issue in the future. Such principles are in our opinion practical fundamentals that both service and reinforce the readiness for members of the organization to engage in and contribute to a positive school community.

In the previous chapter we discussed how teachers could use reflective practices to create positive learning environments for all students. To learn to be reflective is not an easy task that merely requires following a simple prescription. Fred will have to show that he also is a reflective practitioner if he is to be successful in encouraging and supporting other teachers in learning to become reflective and thinking practitioners.

The evidence base is important: to be an effective reflective teacher one should not accept any theory or research on its face value. Rather one should carefully try out new practices in the classroom and then make a judgment – whether to adopt the practice or not, based on sound practice evaluation principles. Any judgment to accept or reject a research finding or theory should be made after systematic implementation and careful evaluation. Systematic implementation means that a teacher makes her best efforts to apply the research or theory in its entirety.

Consider Cynthia. She has been teaching in Fred's school for the last five years and she is frustrated with Tom's behaviour. She says that she has tried everything but Tom continues to be a huge discipline issue. She wants him permanently excluded from the school. She has just completed some professional development and learnt about a new theory of dealing with student disruption. She tries out the new theory, implements it for a short time and notices that Tom's behaviour does not improve. Discouraged, she blames the theory and says it was a waste of her time. A closer look at what she did however might well show that she failed to apply the theory as the researchers intended when they designed the interventions, and she may well have given up prematurely.

Let's consider a parallel example. A patient is suffering from a bacterial infection. The patient has been prescribed 15 antibiotic tablets and is asked to take one tablet three times a day for five days. The patient takes the medicine as prescribed for the first three days. He notes a significant improvement in the symptoms and decides to stop taking the medicines. The symptoms reappear after five days. The patient then starts taking the left over medicine and finds that the symptoms do not improve. In this example it would be understandable for the patient to blame the medicine or the medical practitioner, even though we know that he did not take the medicine as prescribed. Blaming the medicine or the doctor is not only erroneous; it is unlikely to improve the symptoms!

A careful appraisal means that when we evaluate the effect of an application of a new theory in our class, we must have a sound understanding of the underlying theory and evidence on which the theory is based. Moreover, we should know what we can realistically expect to change as a result of its implementation. In Cynthia's case she wanted to see an improvement in Tom's behaviour, tearing up work sheets. She needed to have realistic expectations of what change she can expect, for example as to whether the behaviour of tearing paper might disappear immediately or gradually.

This chapter is based on a well-known adage that *the best time to implement behavioural strategies is when there is no behaviour problem.* It is most effective to be proactive and preventative rather than reactive, in regard to disruptive behaviours. Moreover, such strategies allow us to create an environment where everyone enjoys learning and so then there is no need for our students to misbehave, no need for controlling behaviour. It makes for well-being and happiness all round. The key principles presented in this chapter have been well validated by a wide body of research (Dev, 1997; Glasser, 2007; Klem & Connell, 2004; Monahan et. al., 2010). Translation of these principles into evidence-based classroom practices is the most assured way of creating positive learning environments for all students. Such environments innately encourage students to constructively and responsibly learn cooperatively, naturally minimizing disruptive or destructive anti-social activities.

PRINCIPLE 1: MOTIVATION AND ENGAGEMENT

It is well established that motivation and engagement are essential ingredients for effective learning. Motivation offers a cogent explanation for behaviour (Guay et al., 2010). There is an extensive body of research that shows that students when highly motivated are less likely to drop out, perform better academically, are better adjusted to school, are more likely to feel confident about their ability to learn new material, and behave better in the classroom (Dev, 1997; Guay et al., 2010; Lai, 2011; Lumsden, 1994). We also know that keeping all students motivated and engaged can be challenging for many teachers. However, there are strategies that teachers can learn to understand and use to enhance student motivation and ultimately student engagement. Prior to learning about what can be done to improve student motivation, we do well to understand why some students have poor motivation.

Student motivation can be placed in two categories: extrinsic and intrinsic motivation. Extrinsically motivated students engage in a task purely to earn rewards or to avoid punishment (Dev, 1997). These rewards could range from students getting stickers, candies or public recognition. Example of a punishment could be privileges being taken away from students, such as asking a student to stay in the class during recess to complete the work that he or she has not completed. Intrinsically motivated students engage in a task because they are motivated from within to do an activity. They engage in a task because they like it, they are curious about doing it, and enjoy the act of doing it. Intrinsically motivated students typically have a greater degree of interest in the task. They will engage in the task because they are excited by its challenging nature (Dev, 1997). Students who are intrinsically motivated are likely to do better academically and socially when compared to students who are extrinsically motivated. Some researchers have even argued against using extrinsic motivation as it can lower student achievement and commitment to the task, when there are no rewards or contingencies in place (Brooks, Freburger, & Grothreer, 1998; Dev, 1997). It has also been argued that while extrinsic motivation can sustain or improve productivity in the short term, it reduces the chance that the task will be sustained in future (Brooks et al., 1998).

A student, who is extrinsically motivated, performs an activity because he or she expects a reward at the completion of the activity, rather than experience a specific sense of satisfaction for the act of doing the task. Clearly intrinsic motivation is to be preferred over extrinsic motivation. However, motivating someone intrinsically is no easy task. As educators, we do well to identify those activities in which all students would like to intrinsically engage and succeed. Cynthia's interaction with Tom so far, has been negative. Cynthia, in one way, might demonstrate that she is genuinely interested in working with Tom by drawing upon interests that motivate him. This requires sharing time with Tom that focuses on his interests, activities and routines. She might also find it useful to spend time with his parents and friends in order to get a better picture of Tom's interests, preferences and abilities.

Setting up and creating motivating and engaging tasks requires purposeful and careful planning for each student. Understanding all our students requires focused

Questions for reflection

Do you know the interests of the majority of your students (most importantly a student like Tom)? Do you have a profile of "what motivates each student" and "what does each student want to be when he or she grows up"? If yes, how do you use this information in your teaching? If not, how would you like to gather this information and use it when teaching?

effort. This is best done early in the school term so that the majority of classroom activities can be linked to students' interests and routines, setting up good patterns and habits from the very beginning rather than having to modify and remediate. Teachers who are most successful in creating engaging classrooms are those who learn about their students really well right from the start. These teachers quickly come to appreciate the individual psychological and intellectual needs of their students. They take an interest in their students' subculture. They familiarize themselves with the movies and TV programs that their students watch, the sport their students play, and how they spend their weekends and holidays. Such information offers invaluable basics for a teacher to use in creating a motivating and engaging classroom.

How well do you typically go about creating engaging classrooms? You may find it useful at this stage to rate yourself on a scale from 1 to 10 – where 1 stands for never and 10 stands for always.

In my class, students

a. participate in interesting activities?
b. succeed rather than fail?
c. work co-operatively alongside their peers?
d. have choices and some degree of autonomy? and class activities are built upon what students,
e. already know, and
f. can relate to in real life.

If you find there are some areas where you (or your students) would rate you below 5, then you should seriously think about what you can do to improve your ratings (and eventually your teaching).

While creating an interesting activity sounds simple, as teachers we all know it is by no means an easy task to achieve day in, day out. It requires teachers to design activities which not only motivate one student, but the majority of the students in a class. Back to Cynthia: she has spoken to Tom and she knows that Tom likes watching Pokémon cartoons. He also has a big collection of Pokémon cards. Other students in the class also have some interest in Pokémons. Cynthia can use this information about her students and Tom to design numeracy and literacy lesson plans around Pokémon characters. Tom, in fact, could actively help the teacher with the teaching activities. Interesting activities could also be designed by using a mystery approach. Students are presented with contradictory information and they have to solve the mystery to find the right answer. An example of such an activity would be when a teacher describes a mystery creature by presenting limited information about an animal (e.g., an extinct species) and then students have to find out what the animal is, based on the information given by the teacher and by undertaking more research. This activity not only enhances student motivation, it also encourages co-operation amongst students to solve the mystery. The difficulty of the task could be increased or decreased based on the grade level or abilities of students.

The second fundamental consideration in creating a motivation centred classroom is to ensure that all students, including those who may have a disability, have a chance to succeed in the task. Sometimes we design tasks that are too easy for some and too difficult for other students. The task should engage all students and ensure they are adequately challenged but at the same time, they can succeed. This requires us to think of a variety of activities for each lesson. Students who are highly competent can do advanced activities. Low ability students, on the other hand, need to do activities appropriate for their capability level. Advanced primary grade students (in the above example) could be asked to do research on reasons for extinction of dinosaurs. Low ability students, on the other hand, could draw their favourite dinosaur and describe two main characteristics of it. By the way, don't forget that children have wonderful ideas and imaginations, so we need to encourage them to suggest appropriate activities!

The third consideration relates to students working in small groups in a 'co-operative learning' environment. Children learn best when they have opportunities to clarify their questions, interact with others, and explain their understanding to others. Systematically designed co-operative learning activities enable the achievement of all three. In a co-operative learning environment, each student is responsible for his or her learning as well as the learning of other group members. The teacher has an important role, to ensure that all groups are working well and that each group has access to all the resources necessary to participate in the learning activities. Most significantly, co-operative groups allow each member to benefit from sharing their understanding of the topic with their group and with the whole class.

Allowing students to make choices and therefore act with some degree of autonomy in class activities, represent good strategies that will enhance student participation. Students can be given choices in the way they receive information about a new concept, and also equally importantly, in the way they can demonstrate their learning. For example, students could be given a choice to find out the reasons for the extinction of dinosaurs by reading about the topic in books, researching it over the Internet, or by watching a documentary. They can demonstrate their understanding of the concepts by writing an essay, doing a role-play, drawing an extinct jungle or through an oral presentation. Students could also be given a choice of working independently, with one other student or in small groups. While this requires a bit of planning from the teacher, the rewards in terms of student participation are likely to make it very worthwhile.

The last consideration in making classrooms engaging requires us to relate teaching to the real life events of our students. Activities that build around daily routines at home and community provide students with an opportunity to apply their learning to real life. Practicality is important for most of us. We do well to remember that students are more motivated to learn about concepts that allow them to solve day-to-day problems.

PRINCIPLE 2: NEED TO BELONG

In taking over the school, Fred soon realised that the majority of students in school were feeling disconnected from any sense of community, that is, they lacked a sense of belonging. The students' responses to a school survey indicated that they did not like their teachers, had limited interest in attending the school, and found the schoolwork boring. These are the classical signs of disconnection and disaffection (Klem & Connell, 2004; Monahan, Oesterle, & Hawkins, 2010). Research indicates that around 40% to 60% of high school students report being disconnected from school (Klem & Connell, 2004). It also shows that students who feel well connected to schools manifest fewer behavioural problems, have better academic outcomes, are committed to learning, and complete their homework. Benefits from being connected to school also include a reduced tendency to engage in violent and delinquent behaviours, drug and alcohol abuse, and a reduced likelihood to engage in inappropriate sexual activity at an early age (Klem & Connell, 2004; Monahan, Oesterle, & Hawkins, 2010).

A feedback loop exists between school connectedness and disruptive behaviour (Monahan et al., 2010, p. 4): "Low school connectedness increases the chance that students develop conduct problems, which further lowers a sense of school connectedness, which in turn leads to more conduct problems." This gives Fred a clear perspective on understanding what is driving problems related to pupil behaviour at his school, and why an authoritarian system is unlikely to offer a long-term constructive solution. The question is, what can Fred do to enhance student connectedness to his school?

Looking at the attributes and learning of schools with high degrees of connectedness provided invaluable directions for Fred. These included the following attributes (Klem & Connell, 2004; Monahan et al., 2010) against which we encourage you to rate your school on a scale of 1(not at all) – 10 (always): these include

- high academic standards for all students,
- a relationship between educators and students which is positive and respectful,
- an environment that is safe both emotionally and physically,
- positive and proactive classroom management strategies are used,
- tolerant discipline policies are used,
- co-operative learning activities are used prominently.

When translating this research into practice in his school, Fred knew he would need to ensure that all students be set appropriate academic standards (National Research Council and Institute of Medicine, 2004). He instigated a policy where students with similar abilities were not grouped together, but rather distributed heterogeneously across small groups. Students who are not doing well academically were thus provided with support to enhance their academic achievement, while brighter students consolidated their understanding from 'teaching', something we as teachers all regularly experience. Learning activities focused on students working co-operatively in their small groups foster mutual respect, and social responsibility.

Fred went on to ensure that the school promoted learning activities closely tied to the lives of students, with practical opportunities for hands-on activities associated with learning new and different concepts. Most importantly, each student was given an adviser with whom they were encouraged to talk over any problems or frustrations in or out of school. These pastoral carers were selected on the basis of being good listeners, supported by training level 1 counselling skills that include effective listening and problem solving. It was recognised as essential for these to have a capacity to build ethically responsible relationships of unconditional positive regard, and trust, so students could safely share personal stories and frustrations and where confidentiality was assured.

Students who are well accepted by their peers and have close friends in school are less likely to get disconnected from school. On other hand, students who are harassed and bullied by their peers would find it difficult to connect to school. Having parents who value education and are actively involved in their education, and close friends in the school cumulatively act as strong buffers against school disconnectedness. In order to translate this research into practice, Fred decided to organize informal monthly meetings with parents. This was an important step toward re-instigating new life into the organization of the school as a learning community.

Fred saw this as an effective way of also helping parents to feel connected to the school. He knew that students generally do not form a connection to a school to which parents remained disconnected. Teachers, including Cynthia, collected email contacts of all parents in the school. All teachers agreed that frequent interactions with parents about general class activities were necessary. Some teachers agreed to send out fortnightly emails to parents of all the children enrolled in their classes, keeping them informed about what and how their children were doing well in the school.

PRINCIPLE 3: CHOICE THEORY IN THE CLASSROOM

How often are we teachers frustrated by students who will not do the work we would like them to do in the way we would like them to do it? This was a huge problem in Fred's school. Teachers complained that when a student was asked to comply, he or she inevitably became a discipline problem. Understanding and implementing choice theory as a basis for structured intervention (Glasser, 2007) was an important facet Fred introduced to deal with these issues and became a more generalised approach to 'school behaviour'. Choice theory gives a constructive framework and techniques for dealing with such behaviours, thus avoiding significant discipline issues.

School communities are typically made up of disparate groups of people thrown together by geography and common needs: having the best environment to allow their children to learn to live well. However, a large number of people don't always naturally get along with one another to the extent they would really like. It requires some time and effort to build a coherent social community. But fundamental to such an effort is the need for a substantive well-validated theoretical framework to guide the building of a positive culture.

Choice theory offers just such a basis for understanding why we get along better with some and not with others. People have a tendency to want to see others conform to their own particular way of thinking. We cope with others who are different by exercising what Glasser calls, seven 'deadly habits': these are, criticizing, blaming, complaining, nagging, threatening, punishing, bribing, in order to control. While such strategies might give us a sense that we win in the long term, Glasser suggests they can all be quite destructive of relationships and wellbeing.

If we want to build a constructive community around ourselves, we need to stop using the deadly self defeating habits and replace them with what Glasser tells us are the seven positive and 'caring habits': supporting, encouraging, listening, accepting, trusting, respecting, and negotiating differences. The act of choosing appropriate ways of dealing with a conflicting situation is the key to choice theory. It is important to understand that the seven deadly habits are not communicated only by the words that we use, but also by actions and non-verbal modes of communication (e.g., frowning, ignoring).

Choice theory applies to all people, including teachers and students. Teachers can benefit considerably by becoming aware of the seven deadly habits when interacting with their students and colleagues. Students also do well if they learn to treat other peers with respect by using caring habits when interacting with them. The golden rule of choice theory is that "I am going to treat you the way I would want to be treated, whether you treat me this way or not". Teachers can make significant changes if they model and encourage the alternatives throughout each school day.

Another direct application of choice theory in the classroom is to introduce a competence-based approach to the curriculum for all students. Students come to dislike school if they expect they are going to fail in a subject or get very poor grades. Choice theory suggests how this situation must change. If we know that a student will either fail in the subject or get very poor grades, then this is something that needs to be addressed early. Sometimes the task is too difficult for the student or he or she may not have mastered it before an exam. Scores in the exam would be poor. This typically results in alienation from and rejection of the school (including peers and the teacher) by the student. Such rejection is likely to be displayed through unacceptable behaviours.

In a school that uses choice theory, students are challenged by asking them to do a task that is neither too easy nor too difficult; they are also supported to meet the challenge. Students try their best to achieve beyond mere competence. Some teachers would argue that not all students 'can do' competent work. Glasser, however, would argue that all students 'can do' competent work or even better, if they are told that nothing less will be accepted. Most importantly, students are told that they will be provided with all the necessary support for them to be successful at performing a challenging task. The extra support could mean extra time in completing the task or remedial support on an academic task. It could also mean moreover, setting up a modified curriculum that is based on thinking skills rather than on rote memorization, and constructive notions of deep learning.

The theory and the implications of this approach for schools can be seen clearly in Glasser's (2007 p.?) own words:

> I realize that many teachers do not believe such a school [where choice theory could be used] would be possible with the students they are asked to teach, many of whom seem to have given up trying. They do not realize that low grades and external control have, over a long period of time, caused many dropouts. But when these obstacles are removed and all the students begin to do competent work, this positive effort can lead beyond school to raising the expectations and the effort of the whole community.

Fred decided to apply choice theory school wide. All teachers in his school were provided with professional development and subsequent consultancy support on choice theory, with special assistance for implementing it at the classroom level. Students were also given sessions and workshops on choice theory, encouraging them to apply it in their day-to-day interactions with their peers and teachers. The golden rule "I will treat you the way I would like to be treated" is not just something written on the school walls: it was taught through modelling top down, by the Principal, teachers, class activities and role plays.

PRINCIPLE 4: RESILIENCE IN THE CLASSROOM

Children will often face situations and experiences they will find difficult to cope with and many but not all survive. Such situations might include parental abuse or peer abuse. An example of such a situation within a school could be bullying in the playground by one or more students. These incidents may not come to the notice of schoolteachers and a student may continue to suffer. Most schools have anti bullying policies to protect children. However, such situations in and outside the class cannot be completely eradicated. One personal quality that enables students to deal effectively with such situations is by developing resilience. Resilience is defined as the ability to bounce back. It is the process of, capacity for, or outcome of successful adaptation despite challenging or threatening circumstances (Masten & Coatsworth, 1998).

Harvey and Delfabbro (2004) stress that significant risk factors within schools and outside schools will continue to exist and it is naïve to expect that children can be shielded completely from the pressure and situations previously described. In order for resilience to develop, a person must first be exposed to an adverse situation and risk, rather than being protected from the adverse situation. Resilience is considered an active process and people who are successful in being resilient are those who can manipulate their environments and thus become insulated against the negative effects of the adverse events (Harvey & Delfabro, 2004).

An examination of research (Harvey & Delfabro, 2004; Masten & Coatsworth, 1998; NCH, 2007) suggests that there are a wide variety of factors (within child, family and the community) that contribute to a person becoming resilient. The factors range from strong social networks, a committed mentor or other person from outside the family, positive school experiences, a sense of mastery and a belief that one's own efforts can make a difference, the ability, or opportunity, to 'make a difference' by helping others. In addition, being aware that to be excessively sheltered from challenging situations will not provide opportunities to develop coping skills. One factor that is paramount in making a person resilient, is the presence of at least one unconditionally supportive person (parent, teacher or a mentor).

Other researchers (e.g., Daniel & Wassell, 2002) have provided a slightly different but related framework, in describing what factors may contribute to a person becoming resilient. They describe intrinsic and extrinsic factors in building resilience. The intrinsic factors are: a secure base (having a sense of belonging and safety), high self-esteem (a sense of self worth and competence), and a sense of self-efficacy (an understanding of personal strengths and limitations). The extrinsic factors include positive school experiences, access to at least one supportive person, and access to wider supports network (such as family and friends).

The research above provides a useful framework that schools can adopt and share to help students become more resilient. Schools must make sure that there is at least one supportive person each child can go to in time of crisis. That person must be someone the student trusts, and who will maintain the confidentiality of information shared, but will also assist them by teaching skills or providing additional resources to face the situation. Schools must also ensure that each student develops a high, but true sense of efficacy in his or her abilities in general, but most importantly in dealing with the particular situation. All students can benefit substantially from learning specific strategies to deal with difficult situations, through which they gain a stronger sense of self-efficacy.

Research has identified that families and peers can play a significant role in promoting resilience in students (Harvey & Delfabro, 2004; Masten & Coatsworth, 1998; NCH, 2007). A close partnership between families and schools effectively facilitates families in understanding what skills each child requires to deal with difficult situations. Families need to be assured that schools will do whatever possible to prevent adverse events (e.g., bullying). They need to be adequately informed to deal competently with the situation, and consider it necessary to enlist the family's (carers or significant others) support for the student. Similarly peers could also work in supporting each other to face adverse situations.

In terms of turning around the failing school, Fred decided to translate the research on resilience into practice by ensuring that each student had an opportunity for resilience training. The local department of education provided funding to conduct the training at the school. Fred also employed a full time social worker (Sue). Her main responsibility was to ensure that students feel safe in the school and could contact her if there are any issues that bother them.

TEACHING STRATEGIES THAT WORK FOR EVERYONE!

Fred's school is slowly changing. The school work force has completed several professional development activities. They now have a whole school policy based on some of the fundamental principles of creating engaging classrooms. The impact of renewed school policy has started showing some positive impact. The number of discipline issues has significantly declined but there is still some way to go.

Fred is aware that it will take some time before he can confidently say that the school has changed. Sue, who also attended all of the PD activities, noted that in almost all of the PD sessions the speakers talked about co-operation and co-operative learning. Having spent time in many classrooms across the school, she noticed that even though all staff valued co-operative learning, there is scope for developing this further. She suggested to Fred that it would be of great value to the whole school if a PD could be arranged on co-operative learning (CL).

COOPERATIVE LEARNING

During a full staff meeting Fred regularly asked whether staff would like to have a PD on co-operative learning. Cynthia objected, "We already have had many of these, so why another one?" Kate, who just started at this school a few months ago, said that she learned about CL during her initial teacher training at university. She said that she had found CL to be one of the best strategies to create engaging classrooms. Sue went on to say that she had recently read an article claiming that co-operative learning is one of the most researched strategies and its impact on students has always been positive (Johnson, Johnson, & Stanne, 2000). Students taught using co-operative learning methods typically like the subject material, the teacher, and the school. Most importantly students' academic achievement across different subjects and grade levels is higher in co-operative learning classrooms (many students can get highest grades) compared to students who are taught using competitive methods (where only one student can get the highest grade).

Most importantly, students have less frequent disruptive behaviours and form better friendship with their classmates working in co-operative groups compared to traditional classrooms (where either students work in small groups or work individually) (Johnson, Johnson, & Stanne, 2000). Having heard so much about the benefits of CL, most staff agreed that it would be worthwhile to organize a PD on CL. This is what Fred wanted to hear and he agreed to organize it.

There is some misconception in the education community about what CL is. Some educators believe that when children work in small groups they learn co-operatively. In reality, co-operative learning is much more than working in small groups: there are five key principles to determine if someone is using co-operative learning or not (Johnson & Johnson, 1999). A useful acronym we can use to remember the five principles (PIGSF (*Pigs Fly*) (D. F. Brown (1992)) is:

85

P – Positive interdependence
I – Individual accountability
G – Group and individual reflection
S – Small group skills
F – Face to face interaction

Positive interdependence is one of the fundamental characteristics of co-operative learning. It maintains that the group cannot be successful unless each member of the group contributes toward the success of the group. In other words, each member needs to do his or her part for the group to be successful. In a traditional group activity, some members of the group will complete the task while others may not have contributed anything. If a member of the group is finding it hard to do the activity, it is the responsibility of the rest of the group members to ensure that the person completes the task assigned to him or her. If the person fails in the task, the whole group fails in the task. Teachers can promote interdependence by providing resources that need to be shared to complete the task or by assigning the group to a task that cannot be completed unless each group member contributes.

Individual accountability – is assigned to each member of the group as individual tasks are assigned to the group. Each person must do something related to the group task. A person should also ideally receive recognition for the work he or she completed. Teachers could do this by asking each person to identify the individual contribution of each member. Another way this can be managed is by asking all members of the group to do a 'composite' test. While each member will get an individual score for how well he or she does in the test, the group's overall score will be a total of all of its group members' scores on the test. The group has a vested interest in ensuring that each member gets as high a score as possible on the test, because a poor group score reduces the overall ranking of the group.

Group and individual reflection – after completing a task, group members must spend time in evaluating the performance of the group and of each member. This phase is critical. Working in close collaboration, the group decides what they did well as a group and how each member contributed to their overall success. If the group does not perform well? Then they need to decide what are future means available to improve their group's performance. This may also be the time to find out ways a member of the group could be assisted to do well in forthcoming group activities. It is absolutely vital that the group does not engage in criticizing one person or ascribing to an individual responsibility for the group's poor performance. The reason any one person has not done well on the task may not only be because of his or her poor contribution, but also because of the limited support provided by the group members.

Small group skills – success in co-operative learning depends on how well group members work in small groups. They need to learn to resolve their conflicts effectively, manage their time so that they can complete the task on time, provide feedback to each other respectfully and decide how the group will complete the task. Many of these skills are not taught in traditional group activities. Effective teaching through co-operative learning requires teachers to explicitly teach necessary small group skills to each member of the class. Each group should be provided feedback on how well it used small group skills. Teachers can also grade students based on how best the groups use small group skills.

Face-to-face interaction – co-operative learning requires students to interact frequently with each other. Such interactions cannot take place if students can't see each other face to face (contrast this to a traditional classroom where students are seated in rows). Eye to eye and knee to knee (EEKK) is a common phrase used to describe how the group should be organised. The EEKK arrangement allows students to pay close attention to what each member has to say. Also, in this arrangement it is very unlikely that a student will be left out of group discussion.

Sue's comment that a majority of teachers in the school were now using CL was 'music' to Fred's ears. He also noted that the majority of students was more engaged with formal learning in the classroom and generally seemed more co-operative. Fred acknowledged noise levels in some classrooms as an issue, but he also pointed out that co-operative learning does require students' interaction and he argued that the rise in this kind of noise that he and others had noticed was 'productive noise'. This was in sharp contrast to what was happening when Fred started at the school. A majority of students were mostly off task. Few, if any students had enjoyed class activities, many disturbed other students, and some teachers resorted to yelling for attention and/or shouting from frustration. Now, clearly, classes were becoming more interesting and motivating for most students – a welcome change that many teachers admitted they had been waiting for a long time.

The teachers agreed as the meeting came to an end. They were less stressed. Sue insisted that she for one, felt very happy that the classroom culture was slowly changing and most students were now enjoying school. Sue knew that there were some other teaching strategies that could further improve the classroom environment and students' academic and social outcomes. The two strategies that she wanted to mention, as she had recently heard about them from a colleague in another school, were called *differentiated instruction* and *peer tutoring*. She proposed that the school could benefit immensely by looking at these and other strategies related to an inclusive approach to education.

Sue regularly shared her enthusiasm about the strategies with colleagues and asked Fred if more PDs could be arranged. He agreed that these strategies would be good for the school but decided to give his staff a break from any more PDs in the current year as he wanted to see a consolidation of what the school had already learned through the recent PD sessions. Professional development on differentiated instruction and peer tutoring it was agreed, would form part of the planned PD programme for the next year.

A REFLECTION: CHOICE, CHANGE AND COMMITMENT

Liam came to this school one year ago when his son had verbally abused a teacher. Many things have now changed. School seems to be a much better place, where teachers care about each student and are trying their best to see that that discipline issues do not arise. Members of staff understand the value of prevention and the value of having a whole school policy to deal with school behaviour. Liam's son told him that he now enjoys coming to school. Liam doesn't avoid other parents any more, like he had in the past when he'd felt embarrassed about his son's behaviour.

Liam's son recently completed a survey about the school, and his responses are in stark contrast to what they were a year ago. He likes his teachers and the school! He is no longer bullied or singled out any more. Three things that Liam's son felt had made the huge difference in the school were:

1. to have a person like Sue that all students can trust in the sharing of personal stories;
2. teachers who treat all students with respect and make learning fun; and,
3. the principal, Fred, who is very supportive of teachers and students. He even plays volley ball with Liam's son.

When asked, Liam confessed the school was far from perfect, but he believed that levels of commitment and change had been profound. He mentioned how most of the factors we have described in this chapter had driven a turnaround and started a journey towards school improvement that he was certain would continue in the following academic year.

Questions for reflection

A number of research based strategies were presented in this chapter. If used on a regular basis, they should reduce or eliminate disruptive behaviours in schools. However, such strategies are not widely used. In your view – why is this not done and what could be done so that such strategies are used more commonly?

CHAPTER 7

LEADING A POSITIVE LEARNING APPROACH IN THE SCHOOL COMMUNITY

OVERVIEW AND KEY CONSTRUCTS

- Intelligent inclusion
- Positive learning behaviour
- Learning leadership
- Integrative management
- Transformative Leadership
- Leaders leading: Affirmation, Aspiration, Inspiration and Realisation (AAIR).

Meet the Cast

Major Characters:

> Fred – the School Principal
> Cynthia – the sceptical Vice Principal
> Eleanor – a new English teacher at Fred's school

Minor Characters:

> Ben – A parent member at the school staff meeting
> Jenna – Another active parent involved in the school project
> Tim, Sam and Anna – Three students from Fred's school, participants in the school project.

Fred, a school Principal strongly committed to serious conceptual thinking whilst also concerned that his understanding is translated into good practice. Short answers are not found here, but if you want a thorough exploration of the basis of best educational theory and practice, read on and be encouraged!

MAKING A START

The first day: Fred entered his new place of work as the 'boss' and really did wonder what he had signed up for and how he was going to manage this school. The weather had made the commute to work a dream. It had been a clear azure sky marking the high point of an early Indian summer. A typical start for the new school year, and just as typically, it followed what had been a damp and disappointing vacation. Was

89

this a sign? The need to stay positive seemed to ripple across the windscreen of the car as he drove down to the town, passing one of many visions of an alternative life opportunity, some framed in a smorgasbord of impressions, others in what seemed a concept-board running segments of scenic beauty and pastoral idyll. The ocean sparkled deep blue in the middle distance.

He stepped through the main entrance door following the sign to his new office while ruminating on what it was school leaders do? Lead? Manage? Teach? Inspire? Judge? Orchestrate? Was he a servant? Tyrant? Dictator? Demagogue? Bureaucrat? Educator? Should a leader spend most of his time mediating between staff? Running a committee – bound collegiate democracy? What about timetabling? He chuckled to himself: that was one task usually delegated to a Deputy – as timetabling was a sure fire guaranteed case of trying to please everyone and always pleasing no-one at all.

So: we must use delegation. It was after all a leader's prerogative. Or on the other hand, was it a necessity for survival, as insisted upon by the Professional Development Trainer at the leadership course he had attended last month.? Delegate or go under, he had been told, and make sure you use distributed leadership; it will serve to unite the school in the process of managing organizational learning. Know your people. Staff. Students. Governors. This idea of leadership had been described as the essential ingredient in leading a successful learning community (read 'school' for the current buzz term, 'a learning community'). Fred wondered. So far to travel, he mused, from theory to practice. He turned past his new desk and sat down heavily on what was a very comfortable, rather plush leather bound chair. Managerial perk.

Yes, all to play for in what was clearly going to be an interesting but long, eventful first year. The main task: get going with the staff and students and involve everyone in a collective learning endeavour. Fred thought of himself as a leader in learning, exercising learning leadership. School was going to be a collective project about learning – for everyone. It meant working with people, through people, and for people. Fred was determined to make this happen. It would, if the well laid plans of his version of the 'reflective practitioner', and the 'thinking professional', were to come to fruition; it would mean working through a series of steps and activities aimed at establishing the idea of learning leadership. He reflected: It would also mean seeking and securing a 'consensual community' sharing in the idea of education as valuing and exercising forms of leadership, and holistically grounded in the work of successful learning. No member of the school community should ever think they had nothing more to learn. The work in a school was a life-long and often automated process akin to breathing, that goes on until the last breath.

This idea of 'learning leadership', Fred realised, is one in which an approach to management and leadership is about building capability to deal with what, in his experience, often seemed to be an increasing number of issues and decisions related to the uncertain, complex, and sometimes the unsolvable dilemmas of day-to-day practice. It was, he muttered to himself, really about *resilience* and *adaptability*, about know-how and see-through. But ultimately, he thought, it was about ideas, and a model of educational management concerned with the production, as well as acquisition, of new knowledge; learning. Learning to learn and personal growth, and overall, personal, intellectual, emotional and social development. Last but by no means least, Fred mused, this also meant a need for the introduction of his own brand of educational practice, and the something he had decided to call 'intelligent inclusion'. This final ingredient, he believed, was in every way the glue that held all the other stuff together. Or maybe the lubricant that kept all of the other parts working in synchronicity. It was, he concluded, all about an understanding of educational management, an endeavour and a process that always remained concerned with enabling *positive learning behaviour*.

As the school principal, or rather Fred corrected himself, the leader of a school community, he felt the acute need to mentally picture the school as an entity. The 'Three-P' mantra he had once composed came to mind; think and re-think he reminded himself: 'people, place, practices'. He stood up, walked over to the window and stared at the scene. The thought was followed by another mantra he kept in mind: the 'Triple-E' for successful management, think: 'equity, efficiency and effectiveness'. But not always, he then paused to emphasise, and repeated to himself, *not always* in that order.

School: a place and an experience, as well as a series of systems and practice, and any number of different group(s) of people; but most importantly, it was bound together by its own character or ethos that reflected a particular culture and ways of working as an organization. It was, he mused, in the end, a picture that seemed to be much more than just the sum of its parts. And this would and should change shape, depending upon points of view, present perspective and current trajectory of development.

Fred felt the need to take ownership of this entity: he needed to believe that the school would be recognized and known as the 'right kind' of 'corporate identity'. In turn, it would in many ways be shaped by his decisions, using ,evaluation of school behaviour, and his style of leadership rather than being abused by accountability-driven evidence-led measurement of school-based performance. But most of all, ,he knew it would always reflect the soul of the school community. He needed to belong and find meaning in being there as an educationist. And so of course did every other member of the school community.

It was this abstract and perhaps some would argue rather fanciful idea of soul, a kind of human quality that Fred nonetheless associated with individuals as well as a community. He believed it was this quality or human character above all else, that mattered most for the work in hand. It was, Fred believed, his primary task to ensure the work of each and every member of the school community was able to make a useful contribution to nurturing and developing this 'corporate soul'. If he succeeded in this, then the school curriculum, construed both as a formal fare of academic knowledge, and fed by an informal diet of social and personal experience, yes he believed, the curriculum would ideally flow in a balanced and consistent way. The school would thrive in ways that reflected a belief in the potential for education: this approach would foster *affiliation* with the school identity, and generate a sense of *well-being, belonging, meaning*, and *purpose* from being part of, and giving back to, something larger and more permanent than themselves. He wished, above all else, to be successful in this endeavour. If his work as Principal was to be remembered, Fred would ideally like to be known for having taken a lead role in creating a 'caring and sharing approach to educational excellence', in a school determined to 'reach the hard to teach' and so to succeed in 'teaching the hard to reach', marking out his school as special, and even perhaps positively unique in its own right.

THE NEED FOR A WHOLE SCHOOL POLICY ON POSITIVE BEHAVIOUR

Fred was standing at the end of the staffroom. The staff had not met him before, and this was their first full school meeting. It was the first time the staff were together in what was going to be a long road ahead, ending in the Christmas Break. The atmosphere in the staffroom at that moment was charged with a tangible crackle of expectancy. The question thrown out by Cynthia, the deputy principal, was in regard to the serious and pressing issue of student misbehaviour.

Well," Fred opined, thinking aloud. "It goes without saying that I'd like to build on the caring I sense around the place, with a positive approach to school behaviour." The last thing some staff wanted was an approach to bad behaviour that was soft, without sanctions that would let too many troublemakers get away with it. Fred continued speaking, referring to Bill Roger's work and the idea of clearly stating a list of rights, roles, relationships and responsibility (Rogers, 1998, 2000, 2003).

"The main aim," Fred continued, "is to work together to ensure an intelligent inclusiveness with collaborative leadership that embraces shared problem-solving, solution-focused, with decision-making method in our work". The whole area of strategic management and policy-making at this time, Fred thought to himself, should reflect the model described by Rayner (2009), as a sharing practice of 'learning leadership'. This model had been presented as part of a wider approach to managing equity, diversity and differences in education, and was built upon the idea of educational management as a particular form of 'integrative management', requiring 'leadership of learning' and the practical blending of 'inclusive and transformative leadership', to realize a positive approach to managing personal and social diversity in education (see Rayner, 2007).

Fred switched on the Computer and moved quickly to a slide of the interactive model he had been thinking about and started his prepared presentation (Figure 1). Talking through the various aspects identified in this model, in turn he emphasized the collective work required in contributing to the development and management of inclusive policy and provision. He argued, rather than announced, that there was a ready-made case example for one such activity: a project managed by a working group aimed at meeting a present need to re-build the approach to behaviour management.

STRATEGIC LEADERSHIP

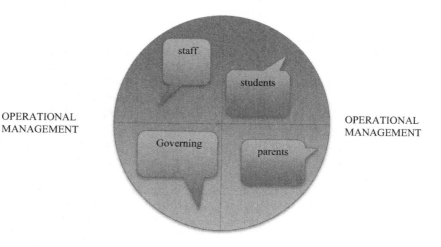

STRATEGIC LEADERSHIP

Figure 1. A learning leadership process

"This," Fred went on to state, "would be the first of several policy groups; it should seek to identify and play to individual strengths (institutional and/or individual), and aim to build upon current success to better deal with systemic weaknesses and operational difficulty. This approach is positive but it does not belie any difficulty; it is consensual but does not deny diversity, or differences, and lastly, it is about consistency that acknowledges complexity. Most importantly, this approach should also emphasize the need for effective communication. None of this means insisting upon uniformity. It does not, for example, mean implementing or operating to a senior management team's corporate diktat. But it does mean signing up to and subscribing to a school ethic that embodies our shared common approach to valuing parity of esteem for every individual, and re-emphasizing the need for sustained educational endeavour. A school at the end of the day is dealing in education. This means working with complexity, uncertainty and change."

"But," Fred insisted, citing Stacey (1992, 1993), "an effective organization is one in which all members of the organization:

- adapt to and help create their situated environments;
- recognise that organisational success flows from contradiction as well as consistency in the work-place;

93

- try to ensure opportunities for success in a self-reinforcing cycle of learning, rather than from explicit vision; and
- realize that transforming, as well as incremental, changes may lie on the route to organisational success.

The work in a school should always be empowering and enabling: it should therefore always return to extolling effective learning, good teaching and positive personal growth."

Fred remembered for the first time being introduced to Bill Rogers' work on behavioural literacy. The idea of 'behavioural snot' still stuck in his mind. Rogers had amusingly struck a chord of empathy in the audience with his caricature. The whiny reluctant learner triggered a vivid image in Fred's mind. Nikki, a precocious 13 years old loomed large to fit with the Rogers' description. Nikki had been a learning experience from his first year in teaching. She had learned to skilfully weave attention seeking into evasive and invasive destructive mis-behaviour. Difficulties at home in an extended family were the frequent explanation. Dad had been in prison and Mum kept on struggling to keep life and family together. There was, nonetheless, a lot of useful stuff in Rogers' practical idea of behavioural literacy (Rogers, 1998). It was worth re-reading (a high compliment from Fred who rarely re-visited a text given the issues of time, work and family).

Fred mused quietly as he glanced over the heads of the group: it was vital to him that members of staff realize they must *see through* a raft of surface behaviours that typically create disruption, and that impede the growth of positive learning. A range of tactics for managing surface behaviour could be usefully employed: deflection, distraction, and his favourite, the 'stuck needle in a record' technique that required slow repetition of the assertions of an angry and disruptive individual. Then, in a calmer setting, there was the empty chair routine and a version of the counselling technique of projecting inner dialogue and what he thought of as the 'there but by the grace of God go I routine'. It was more or less an appeal to empathy and fair play.

Fred turned away from the screen. He thought about the work of Fritz Redl, the American Psychiatrist who devised the term '*surface behaviour*' and a series of techniques for the 'antiseptic treatment' of '*surface misbehaviour*' when working with disturbed adolescents in New York (Redl, 1957). A lot of good stuff to think about in Redl's work, particularly his idea of '*beneath the surface behaviour*'. But Fred had realized that the need to develop shared approaches to behaviour management didn't just stop there.

Fred wanted more; he wished to secure a shared belief in positive learning behaviour throughout the school community that stretches over and beyond the classroom. It was necessarily personal, but it was social too, and it meant engagement with a range of attitudes, with personal feelings, and with what people perceived and believed was their part in the school community. He sighed inwardly as he again glanced around the full room. The school should ideally function as a whole, as a learning community; its aim as an organization would be to nurture a life-long commitment to learning in its members, as well as a shared notion of human dignity, social identity and a positive sense of self. If this were to ever work in practice, members of the school community, including the student body, needed to share in an opportunity to lead and contribute to the educational community. It was Fred's belief that educational management was a specific professional practice. It reflected in turn the particular nature of purposes in schooling as distinctive and different in quality to the many models of business management now dominating the educational establishment. School leadership was first and foremost about the management of learning.

Questions for reflection

Fred is moving towards a whole school policy to create positive learning environments for all.

Does your school have a whole school policy? If yes – Is everyone in your school aware of this policy and its practical implication for students and staff? If not – do you think a whole school policy is needed in your school? What should be included in this policy?

DISTRIBUTING LEADERSHIP

Eleanor jumped involuntarily. It was her turn to speak to the staff. She had agreed to lead a working group charged with review and reform of the school behaviour management policy and provision. This was something of a surprise to her as she was only two years in to working as a Teacher of English. But she had a plan. After a brief discussion with Fred, she had decided to propose a project that looked at producing a more clearly stated set of collaborative protocols and practices for managing behaviour. The group was to be organized in such a way that she would convene a meeting twice a week for a term. The group was made up of four members of the school workforce, three students and a school council member, as well as two parents.

Eleanor began, "We have some really great ways of doing things; we have excellent examples of good will and cooperation, but there are always ways in which we can make a good place even better. I have been doing a lot of thinking. I'd like to facilitate some *'strategic thinking'* that involves *'problematizing'* existing policy. We can then try to create consensus around a series of proposed actions aimed at improving and re-establishing a shared purpose and approach to school behaviour (codes, rights, rules and responsibilities). This would involve looking at ways in which the 'official' values system in the school community might be better communicated across the school organization and embedded in school life."

"The group," she continued to explain, "should ideally aim to move through three stages of what amounts to a project. The first entails the examination of policy, and how the policy might be developed to encourage better learning behaviour. The second is when we should be working to ensure and enable take up of a whole-school code of practice in the wider community. This will involve taking on the challenge presented by the need for consensus building in the community. Thirdly, the group will spend more time looking at issues of fair play, access and opportunity for all students, irrespective of disability or difficulty experienced during the school day. This is a perfect example of an aspect of school leadership that demonstrates how important it is to sustain an inclusive whole school approach to learning, as both an expression of 'institutional behaviour' as a school and as 'learning performance' across school as an organisation."

The New Working Group: Learning about School Behaviour

Eleanor surveyed the group sitting around the table. She held the sheet of paper with a list of questions, or were they in fact issues, with which to begin the group discussion? The long ensuing discussion had identified several very good aspects of current practice in school. A particular area of success was felt to be the anti-bullying initiative that had been running for three years. Jim, a deputy principal, had introduced the idea of an academic researching bullying (Rigby, 2001). The school had introduced a range of provisions across the curriculum, including peer-based counselling, countering bullying as a theme in the curriculum, and the creation of opt-in nurture groups for younger students who self-presented as struggling with one or more aspects of school life. The group quickly agreed there was a great deal that existed in terms of existing school systems; that practice and provision should be affirmed and further reinforced.

Mike, a Physics teacher, was quick to pick up on how this discussion reflected the traditional notion of group formation. There had been some 'storming', followed by a movement toward 'norming' of ideas, perspective and opinion. Eleanor replied that she believed that they would continue to move from identifying strengths in the present system involving what she thought was a process of affirmation, toward a consideration of aspirations and/or goals for further developing the policy. In fact, she argued, she felt that these two stages of activity were continuing to recur in the group discussion, but that this in turn, was paving the way to realizing a need for some inspiration, as problem-posing had begun to encourage an awareness of need for some solutions-led action planning. Ben, a parent member, suggested he play the role of 'secretary' and started to jot down key ideas on the white-board. The group quickly became engaged in the work of searching creatively for ideas and ways forward for developing a better behaviour management policy for the school.

A few months later, Eleanor reflected on how this group had worked so far. Leadership had become a shared responsibility. Each member of the group, in turn, had convened a meeting, having prepared the agenda and chaired the session. This was an invaluable learning experience for all, but especially for the three students involved. It was as if the group had grown its own identity and way of working. Not so different, as Mike had pointed out, to the model of team development devised by Tuckman, that described the sequential forming of a group, followed by conflict, leading to consensus.

Moreover, Eleanor realised, the experience of this group had been more positive than might have been the case if she had used contrived 'icebreakers' and 'warm fuzzies' to manipulate feelings of affiliation, engagement and identity with its membership. It was as if they all shared in an opportunity to make a difference, while at the same time they were all engaged in a meaningful and empowering activity. Eleanor felt sure that the group had in fact experienced the 'coming up for *AAIR*' process she had been loosely following as a leader's plan. This had involved working and re-working four aspects of group activity: managing a mix of *affiliation, aspiration, inspiration and realization.* She was not really sure if this had been because of her own leadership or in spite of it. But what did it matter? The group was working with a buzz and a purpose, and it looked as if they really were going to make a difference in moving school policy forward!

The Working Group: Learning, Belonging and Leadership

Tim, Sam and Anna were all pleased to be involved in this group. They were in their final two years at school and parents had at first been anxious that this involvement would detract from study and the preparation for the all-important final exams. But it had not worked out like that as they all shared in work tasks, and from time to time actually led the group. They expressed how much they had each come to value it as a really good learning experience. A 'buzz' grew for them as the work proceeded. They had all learned something about learning behaviour and learning to lead. Their contribution had included the collection of some very useful testimony about the increase in cyber-bullying and bullying beyond the school gates. Issues had then surfaced about how the school should manage problems associated with alienation and harassment. It was a salutary reminder for all that some members of the community, including parents as well as students and even on occasion, other members of the school workforce were indeed responsible for dangerous and harmful attitudes, behaviours and activity.

At one level, for example, there were clearly articulated problems around sexuality and ethnic identity that despite being so well identified, still required answers to ensure and sustain notions of tolerance, right and wrong. There were no easy options for influencing much of what spilled over in terms of negative attitudes, prejudices, and behaviour from beyond school. A serious issue, for example, was gang culture, but the principle agreed by group members was, start with what can be managed (that is, located within school). The focus should remain on how these influences might be countered within the school community.

All three students assured the group that what happened in school really mattered to them, but it was often what happened after school that caused the greatest effect. One of the students referred to several instances last year of peers caught up in a sex-texting social network closed down by the Police. They all agreed, and argued for, a sense of community that involved more than just a parents' evening, open day, or occasional communications linking school with home and neighbourhood. But everyone agreed: the school in the first instance and for most of the time should be focused upon the behaviour of members of the community in school; and the priority for a behaviour management policy was to foster an attitude to school that would enable excellence in learning.

It was Jenna, one of the two parents in the project group who finally declared the need for some clearly framed statements on how learning behaviour might be defined and in turn how this might be applied throughout school and classroom.

"What is it exactly we think the group is chasing?" Eleanor repeatedly asked this question, realizing that it was in fact a pivotal point in the work of the group. They had reached a first tipping point for re-direction and momentum; there now needed to be a blending of inspiration with aspiration, and this need was reinforced by a shared realization of purpose, and a re-focusing upon direction and outcome.

The Working Group: Decisions, Choice and Change

Jenna seized the moment and asked if she could record the group's agreed statements on the whiteboard. The group agreed to share a set of tasks built around their newly agreed description of learning behaviour. Their work was to target embedding and reinforcing 'learning positive learning behaviour' in an inclusive way across the following areas of school life and community:

1. School behaviour (ethos/climate/culture).
2. Professional behaviour (attitudes/values/knowledge).
3. Student behaviour (attitudes/values/self-perception).
4. Pastoral systems (procedures/protocols/practices).

The group discussions raised insights that outcomes of this work should be ideally incorporated into the school's behaviour management policy. The group agreed that the challenge presented was how to use this policy to foster wider and continuing commitment to and affiliation with the school community? Above all else it should, they reasoned, be used to re-orientate school behaviour management protocols and practice.

The group decided, after reading some of the literature on learning to learn and positive behaviour, that they wanted to integrate the three aspects of behaviour defined by Grimley et al. (2004) to include conduct, emotion and learning. The model was more firmly grounded in class-based learning, and behaviours associated with formal instruction and classroom activity. However, everyone agreed that their very own developing idea of positive learning behaviour was wider and in a sense bigger than this, and while the Grimley et al. model served to help focus upon one important part of positive learning behaviour, there was much more involved. Nonetheless, the group had agreed, the idea of positive learning behaviour should be introduced as an idea, and ideally would lead to further nurturing an important value or ethic to be adopted in the school community.

The following list of key aspects of positive learning behaviour emerged from the group's discussion:

1. The definition of positive learning behaviour included three key sets of personal behaviour comprising emotional behaviour, social conduct, and, learning to learn.
2. The definition of positive learning behaviour included both the personal behaviour associated with learning how to learn, and social behaviours and attitudes associated with involvement in the community.
3. A belief that positive learning behaviour is participatory and reliant upon personal capability (potential for growth) and adaptability (key attributes of resilience and style);
4. An appreciation that activity characterized by a clearly developed action-bound focus, in terms of agreed goals essential for the learner (and others involved in the learning activity), was necessary to cultivate and grow positive learning behaviour;
5. A positive learning approach required a carefully orchestrated balance between capability (personal resources) and challenge (learning task or demands);
6. A positive emphasis was crucial in the management of behaviour; and, in terms of behaviour schemes, systems and protocols, a response to failure, intervention, support, and a practical policy of 'no blame', thereby moving away from a pathology-based causality and deficit-bound culture;
7. An attitude to be encouraged in the school workforce as part of an acculturation of positive behaviour in terms of encouraging personal subscription to a professional ethic that aims to offer encouragement for learners in taking appropriate risk-taking responsibility, whilst also adopting an expectation for a positive individual engagement and participation in community life;
8. The idea of locating every individual in a school-wide conception of a 'learning zone', integrating both the *personal* level (attention, concentration, raised awareness of autotelic activity or flow) with a corresponding emphasis upon positive, appropriate kinds of *social* interaction (expression, articulation, communication, place, time and/or media) to produce positive learning behaviour.

The next step agreed to by the group was to begin mapping out the work specifically required to introduce and reinforce positive learning behaviour in the school. The list included a set of ways and means as well as key indicators for use in orienteering change and mapping out a way forward.

The group issued the following operational statement and agreed that Eleanor should present this to the senior leadership team. The key issue to be raised at this time was how to secure some additional resource to operationalize the policy after it was presented. The group felt it essential that some time and support should now be extended to help make change happen. The work it was agreed should:

1. From the outset involve a whole-school approach, meant for implementing an inclusive policy for managing pupil behaviour and sustaining an inclusive organizational culture.
2. Reflect inclusive levels of engagement and participation in the operation of change management and the re-affirmation of collective beliefs, values and attitudes toward behaviour on the part of all members of the school community (this importantly should involve staff, students, parents, governors and other stakeholders in the school community).
3. Contain and enshrine a key reference point (rule book /code of conduct) to be adopted by the community, supported by a reinforced working set of systems and structures in the organization (a knowledge network framing pastoral care; access points for advice, resource and intervention embedded within the community; and most importantly, a series of supports for learning structures across the academic and professional development curriculum).
4. Ensure that all members of staff have another member of staff (peer) who can actively support and advise them in matters of behaviour management.
5. Link this work to the review and maintenance of knowledge networks and continuing support for professional learning in the school community.
6. Seek to explore ways in which to develop pupil involvement in learning 'positive learning behaviour' and for sustaining 'positive behaviour management' (peer support schemes, anti-bullying work, community decision-making).
7. Target and co-ordinate an extending programme of community participation events such as school-home networking and support groups, mentoring provision, and fund raising (involving parents, voluntary agencies, community groups).
8. Further develop outreach, inter-agency collaboration, and contribute to inter-school partnership and knowledge networking.

So the group was moving forward in what Eleanor felt was the best way possible and the process had ensured everyone was on the same page and on board. They agreed that the approach of positive learning was the way to go, ensuring activity that was useful, relevant and meaningful. It included addressing the issue of criteria for assessing emotional and behavioural development as part of a new approach to 'learning behaviour'. This was to replace the existing emphasis on sanctions, penalties and a 'three strikes and you are out' scheme that worked as a sliding scale ladder to exclusion: a new approach agreed to as might prove more effective in an inclusive approach to managing behaviour in the school setting. One example of such assessment, Eleanor suggested, could be found by re-visiting the assessment piloted by Grimley et al. (2004).

This approach had been publicized by the Qualifications and Curriculum Authority (2001) in the UK and used in a wide range of school settings as part of an approach to improving classroom behaviour (Grimley et al., 2004). It might, if used carefully, serve to provide a firm basis for developing some wider ranging forms of assessment, and link to subject-based curricula in reinforcing a proposed approach to learning positive behaviour. The next step was to wait and see what the response was from the senior leadership team.

Questions for reflection

You notice that Fred's school is not only moving towards designing a new policy – it also considers the way the policy needs to be implemented. In your school, what attempts are made so that a policy is successfully implemented? What lessons can we learn from the scenario above that would lead to the successful implementation of a policy?

DEALING IN DIVERSITY: CONSENSUAL COMMUNITY AND INTELLIGENT INCLUSION

The introduction of change management, targeting the school behaviour policy, was the first in a two-step affair. Fred believed he had to follow this up quickly. He saw a need to set up a second project targeting educational inclusion and diversity in the school community. It was this part of his first year's work at the school which in his own mind had the farthest-reaching implications for the school community. Fred want to stay true to his first principles, which included a deeply held belief in leadership integrity, and an equally deep seated opinion that *charismatic* examples of transformational leadership, (what Fred perceived to be an exaggerated valuing of the lone leader) were ultimately damaging to an educational community; and thirdly, that he wished to pursue a form of leadership described by some as 'transformative'. It was this approach which included the ideas associated with learning leadership and inclusive leadership proposed by Rayner (2007, 2009, 2011).

Fred turned to face his Deputy, a sanguine but sometimes cynical long serving colleague, Cynthia. Fred had been trying to convince Cynthia for over a half an hour that the ideas previously mentioned had worth and intrinsic value. Fred wanted her to consider dipping into the related literature. He cited, for instance, the recent Handbook edited by Shields (2011), entitled '*Transformative Leadership: A Reader*'.

He continued to argue with Cynthia, explaining that he thought the way forward should involve emphasizing a blending of theory and practice in a pragmatic, knowledge-led approach to educational pedagogy and continuing professional development. More importantly, such an approach would help encourage people to engage with and involve everyone across the school community in creating, what he called a 'consensual community'. Cynthia challenged him, asking pointedly, "What on earth does that phrase really mean?"

"Consensual community presumes," Fred grinned, picking up on his first words to continue, "the social and psychological coalescence, and co-construction of a new set of shared beliefs and values will mark out the school ethos, organizational culture, and form the basis of a school community. This should ideally include opportunities for everyone involved in the school to experience and nurture a positive sense of belonging, to develop a pride in their/our work, and, their/our individual contribution to this work. It also would ideally imply a sense of certainty, security and safety associated with the ways and means adopted in the day-to-day running of the teaching, learning and human relations taking place in the school curriculum. In such a school, everyone without exception has a part to play!"

"This idea then means taking the traditional notion of a learning organization and converting it into an educational endeavour that produces something I like to call the 'learning game'. It means exchanging some of the business and commercial values that I understand reside at the heart of much of the literature theorizing organizational learning, and translates it into an educational model, with an appropriate focus on pedagogic practice, learning as a process, and knowledge as a co-constructed product. The end game is to 'make meaning' and 'exercise knowledge management'; that is, we are engaged in the creation, mobilization and transfer of different kinds of knowledge in order to facilitate learning and understanding."

"Creating a consensual community is a crucial means to this end: it is about realizing the management of knowledge creation, the development of the life-long learner and the delivery of inclusive education. This adds up to an education that must offer opportunity in an environment that facilitates personal growth and nurtures education as an empowering enhancement. For me, education is the process intended to *secure* personal growth, *enable* social justice, and, help to *facilitate* well-being as a potential resource for everyone involved with the school community."

"Nice speech," Cynthia said laughing, "but so much of this is, quite frankly, just utopian. What I want to see are tangible signs of success, simple and straightforward things like good exam results." Fred winced. He started again, pointing out that much of what he had described made good sense, positively impacted on educational achievements including exam results, and actually in one way or another was and is a regular and integral feature in education -and is already happening in schools. Fred paused: the idea of transformative leadership was one he wanted Cynthia and the rest of the senior leadership team to seriously consider. It involved revisiting first principles and asking why and what the team was doing as a leadership group rather than only as a management force (aka management farce). Secondly, what did answering the question 'why?' mean for how they worked? Fred, persistently and, he realised, perhaps somewhat doggedly stuck to his point.

Fred faced the small group of senior leaders and hit the pause button. The PowerPoint slide dominated the far wall, summing up the idea of transformative leadership (see Figure 2), as a process of bottom-up-led growth rather than top-down management, accounting driven alchemy or instant transformation.

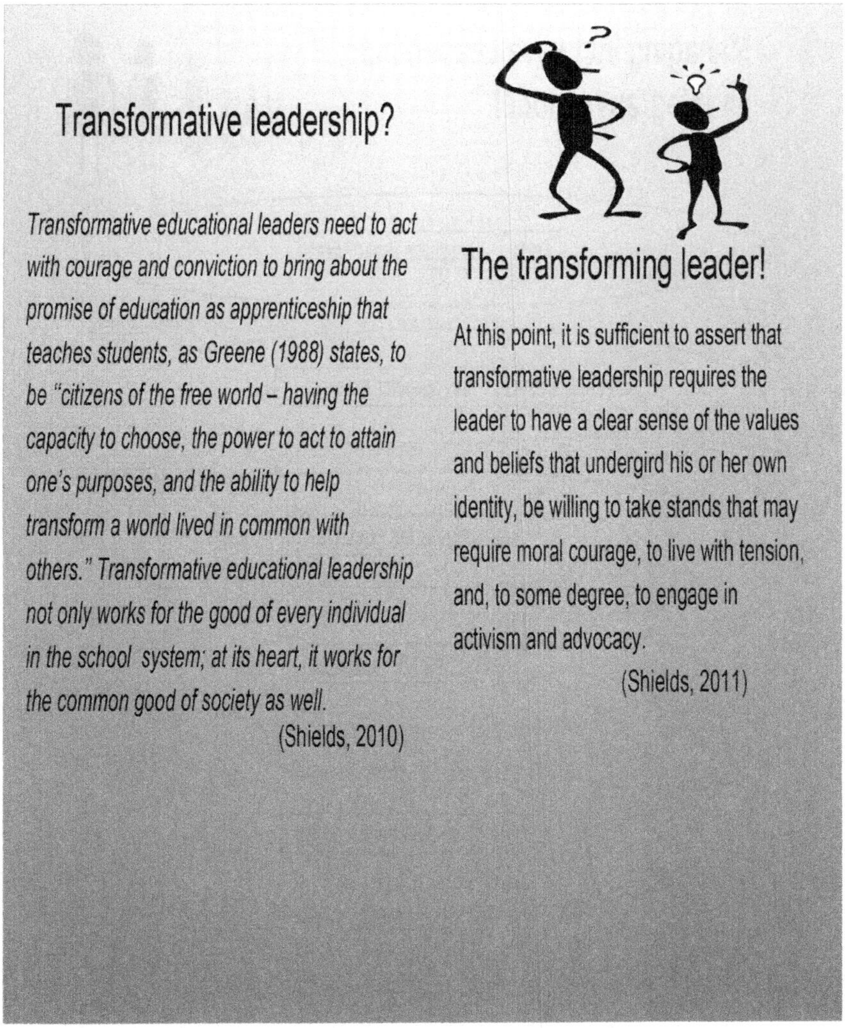

Figure 2. Explaining transformative leaderhsip

"The idea of managing inclusive leadership' as this next slide illustrates (see Figure 3), is a balanced mix of theory and practice in a continuing series of dynamic learning activities, literally represented as the inclusion of various parts of the school organization and community required to work together to sustain a live learning community."

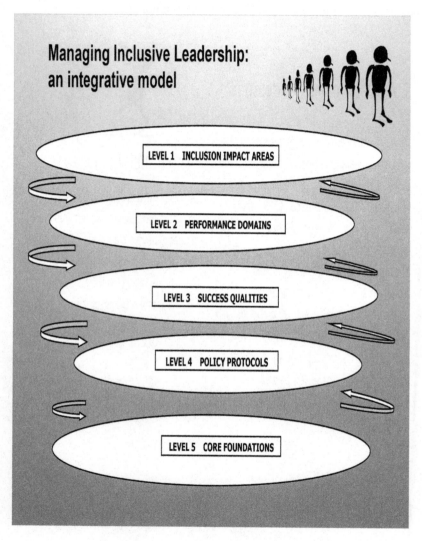

Figure 3. Intelligent inclusion in a consensual community

"The approach," Fred paused before he continued, "requires a pragmatic, applied and integrative method to management that involves working at different levels of the school structure in a related and joined up way. Ultimately, it means ensuring the realisation of outcomes in what is identified on this powerpoint slide as the surface level of impact zones or areas of inclusion in the school organization."

Fred paused and then pointed at the diagram on the screen, and explained, "From beginning with a base level of strategic management, leadership is required in a distributed and focused approach, exemplified in the positive behaviour group being led by Eleanor. We want this to lead to movement, to expand and extend to other aspects and levels of inclusive management as described in the slide (Figure 3), ultimately helping us reach and shape the areas of most visible impact. This occurs in day to day work and the systems we set up to assist this work. For example, networks aimed at the support of learning for students experiencing learning difficulties."

"Similarly, the next slide describes how this approach to inclusion involves seeking to build and work with the idea of a consensual community." Fred turned away to press the switch for the projector. He then carried on with the talk, explaining, "This requires deliberately cultivating an intelligent approach to inclusion that should be embedded in accepting individual differences in people, but emphasizing accommodation of these differences whenever possible, and yet always working and moving towards opportunities for the assimilation of a learning identity with membership of the school (learning) community. This means careful use of a range of artefacts (social media and forms of expression) and assents (agreed viewpoints) in the design and delivery of the curriculum. Similarly, re-clarification of a collective set of values and an acceptance of deeply held beliefs will need to be included in this approach to formal and informal learning. With this in mind, for example, I think we need to carefully re-consider the place and function of school assemblies."

Fred was aware that this approach raised very difficult issues that contradicted some popular approaches considered politically correct, such as, for example multi-culturalism. Nonetheless, he continued by arguing that the process of 'accommodation' required for multi-cultural settings should actually form part of the process aiming at an assimilation of organizational culture and new levels of becoming, belonging and being a member of the school community. An essential action as part of this activity aimed at belonging to the school community, should also lead to an affirmation of a co-constructed, inter-active culture and social identity. Fred almost whispered as he said, "This approach to schooling involves a recurrent thinking about education as dealing in knowledge, personal and social diversity, organizational complexity, social inclusion, and ultimately, equity."

He paused and again pointed to the slide illustrating the inclusive leadership model (see Figure 4). It resembled a mobile chime and he imagined it constantly turning, with the many parts forming and re-forming aspects and perspectives for those both within and beyond the structure. The question of including everyone in appropriate ways and ensuring engagement, involvement, participation, commitment and understanding as the basic work of this inclusive model of leadership. It deals

Embedding Inclusive Curricula: First Base: think structures, agency, learning & understanding

1. Engagement: problematising & reflexive review for focusing intent
2. Participatory Action: distributing & sustaining leadership?
3. Action Zones: making methods, taking steps & managing outcomes
4. Impact Zones: making a difference, enabling success & knowing that ....

- *Learner diversity/ curriculum access*
- *Parity of esteem/participation*
- *Partnership /Service compacts*
- *Support for learning networks*

Figure 4. Exercizing intelligent inclusion

with the many different systems, groups and people in the school, and requires an integrative management of educational diversity in the contemporary school setting. It was also the necessary work required for realising organizational learning in a consensual community.

"This does not mean everyone sharing perfectly shaped and proportional perspectives in perfect harmony, in a state of constant agreement." Fred carried on, almost remorselessly, as staff stared at the diagram. "In fact, the approach should be clearly characterised by an acknowledgement of individual differences, interests and the viewpoints of others, yet integrates these differences in the formation of a new social entity for the individual as a member of the learning community."

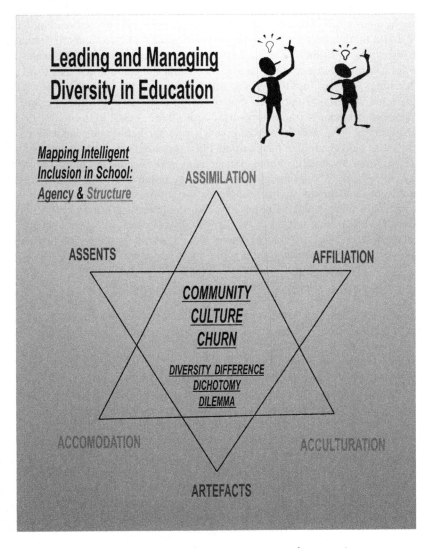

Figure 5. Intelligent inclusion in a consensual community

"Moreover, this means ensuring the staff engage with the work required in making the various parts of this model (see Figure 4) combine in what at the heart of the school's organizational structure, and so community is the mix of these ideas, values, issues and ethics in the churn of day to day activity."

Fred pressed on, declaring that an imperative for educational management involving every member of staff was to facilitate access, engagement, and a widening participation in a full and active learning community. Fred recalled reading Rayner (2007). The model, he recalled, required the blending of two kinds of leadership: 'transformative' and 'inclusive' leadership. Success, he knew, would depend upon an integrated management of this leadership within the community. The focal point was learning. And for Fred this was so much more than the obligatory model of an evidence-led accounting approach that relied on a list of data-smart performance indicators and standards frameworks used to hold the school to account. The latter was not unimportant, and the school bursar's role and school administrative office should not be held cheaply or disregarded, but it represented only one set of tools and associated tasks for an educational management of the school learning community.

Nonetheless, Fred proceeded to summarize the point with renewed emphasis; he wished to re-visit the question of what was the prime function of the school, and in turn, school management: Fred argued that the latter was a pragmatic challenge concerned with means and ends, as well as process and equity; it required that educational leadership and management remain an integral part of the civic or social—as well as academic—function of education.

REFLECTIONS: LOOKING BACK – MOVING FORWARD

Looking back, Fred was not surprised at the resistance to his 'new' style of management in school. He understood the logic of a medical paradigm influencing so many aspects of education: there had always been a long-standing need for remediation of learning difficulties based on a notion of restorative or palliative intervention, which relied in turn on the fundamental act of a contrastive judgment. School had always, it seemed, been largely about sorting out 'pears' from 'apples' and 'sheep' from the 'sheep dog' in order to sort out what was missing.

Fred grunted: this need for labels and categorization, he reflected, clearly did have its place in education, and in the construction of knowledge, understanding and meaning. Categories provided the integral framework for the curriculum, for knowledge and epistemic content. This much was evident, he thought: knowledge was often structured as a set of contrasting binary concepts or elaborated taxonomy. He did hope, however, that schooling was surely not simply and only about curricula designed around this notion of knowledge and linked pedagogy, translated into grading and labelling and setting or norming the learner. Such an approach almost guaranteed a mind-set for deficit-based assessment and the need for winners and losers, competition and league tables, with a basic recipe for failure. The approach was, put simply, about forcing exclusivity via competition, and then seeking accommodation via diagnosis and correction; it was all about putting right what was deemed to be wrong so as to enable a good fit with a proscribed context.

The problem for Fred therefore was mostly one where traditional ideas of education 'norming the standard' approach aimed at re-establishing 'one size for all', and the supply of necessary rejects identified as a kind of epidemiological evidence base demonstrating normal distribution as a validation for the test. What Fred wanted to cultivate was an idea of excellence embracing both this exclusivity and yet something more, reflected in less well established ideas of measuring performance and knowledge acquisition. In a sense this was Fred's vision of an inclusive education, acknowledging, respecting, and coping with individual differences at all levels and areas, as providing a necessary basis for dealing in educational diversity. It presumed for instance that 'capability' might well be a better referencing point than only ability. There was, he thought, a great deal of need for developing new approaches to the measurement of learning in the curriculum, such as 'authentic' assessment.

Discrimination, it seemed, was the traditional and enduring basis of what again was perhaps so often euphemistically called 'entrance criteria' and yet for Fred seemed to be about professional judgments on the 'fit with what we offer' suitability of the 'client'. This was as true, Fred realized, for professionals working in Health, Social Services and School sectors of community care, as it was for teachers in schools. In some senses it was the easy direct way of ensuring a homogenous school community. Differentiation was applied from the outset as a screening mechanism.

Fred sighed: the same set of labelling assessment and selective procedure was widely used in student entry, and the structuring of ability based school classes in the rest of the education system too, including the best fee-paying schools, independent schools, and universities in the country. The irony did not escape Fred. The place of such discriminatory practices existed as deeply embedded social and professional cultures in Education, and were continually reflected in professional attitudes or educational systems – very powerful and certainly deeply embedded!

"Right!" said Fred: again talking to himself, as he paced his office rehearsing some loosely gathered thinking. "So, there was an unfolding yet constant paradox at work in managing educational provision. Education should empower and be socially just, as well as offer routines for the reinforcement of social responsibility; like it or not education is a process of socialization."

This meant that almost, if not entirely by definition, schooling would generate a continuous set of dilemmas, contradictions and tensions in relation to the wider community. It was this selfsame set of issues that re-surfaced when working with social diversity and the challenges associated with equity in the school community (including questions not always asked, but that when addressed, triggered confronting, conflicted values: such as the place and respect given to religious beliefs, or even when at first glance these might seem to be more mundane issues, to do with forms of etiquette, dress, or diet). Should students for example be allowed to wear the hijab? Be granted in-between time in the school lesson for prayer?

Learning, knowing, and teaching; it sometimes seemed to Fred that he was dealing in the delivery of some kind of mystic manna for the human soul. *He wanted to make a difference by ensuring the school was the place that made a difference.* He pondered the place and concept of school. Positive applied psychology: Fred should, he reflected, deal in the right stuff for teaching and learning; the school ethic should be used in turn to reflect and provide an environment conducive to personal growth and learning to learn. It in turn also needed to be a part of the wider community at large if it were to be successful. Never ending ripples within ripples of systemic action moved through the mind's eye as Fred contemplated the need for inter-agency working and community-based support for learning networks and partnerships. New goals for next year's positive learning development loomed larger in his mind.

Fred got up and walked over to the office window. He stared out over the leisure area toward the school's playing fields. He missed playing football. Motive and motivation: well, the work was far from boring; it was stressful, sometimes very difficult, and not without setback and disappointment. So now it was time to move on and meet the senior leadership team, governing body and positive behaviour group in a decision-taking session. Then there was the need to think beyond this year to the next. Truth be told, Fred thought, he actually got an intense buzz from this daily, weekly, term by term, continuing challenge and well, there it was, he realized, he really did love this work, though in teacher circles somewhat perversely, it might not be cool to admit it!

Questions for reflection

"Distributed leadership is a better way to lead school change" – Do you agree or disagree with this statement?

Reflect on the current leadership practices in your school and think of the ways the school leadership team can work with other members of the school community to lead the school to better outcomes for all.

CREATING POSITIVE LEARNING ENVIRONMENTS

What Parents and Teacher Assistants Can Do

OVERVIEW AND KEY CONCEPTS

- Team teaching
- Collaboration and partnership
- Capacity building
- Role of teacher aides

Meet the Cast

Main Characters:

> Cynthia – teacher
> Judy – parent of 10 year old Cameron
> Narelle – a new teacher aide for Cameron
> Kate – a fresh graduate teacher
> Nick – school psychologist

Minor Characters:

> James – a teacher at the school PD.

This chapter takes another and different experience of the school community. We explore here the perspectives of parents and teacher assistants, in an attempt to learn a little more about how everyone plays a part in an inclusive approach to the learning community.

Judy was very anxious. She had just received a phone call from Cameron's school. Cameron was Judy's 10-year-old son, who had just had another bout of his usual behaviour outburst at school. They want her to come and pick him up. This was the 4th time within last three months that Judy has been called to take her son home. She was very stressed with the whole situation and didn't know what she could do about it. While driving to school from work, Judy started asking herself a number of questions: Should I enrol Cameron in another school? Can I lodge a complaint to the Department of Education for the school's inability to handle Cameron properly?

After all, what has happened this year, all of a sudden, to make him start misbehaving so frequently?

On her way to school, Judy had some time to think about the situation. Cameron has got a new teacher, Cynthia, and a new teacher aide, Narelle. Could they somehow be responsible for his disruptive behaviour? Even if they were, who would accept it? She decided to discuss this with Fred, the Principal. Unfortunately Fred was on study leave for two weeks so she had to wait before she could discuss it. He was due back on the coming Monday. Judy arrived at the school. The receptionist knew that Judy would be coming to pick up her son. She told her that Cameron was in the 'sickbay' and she could take him home. "Would you like to talk to Mr. Thomas?" asked the receptionist.

"No, Thank you. But can I get an appointment to see the school principal sometime? But I know he is not here this week". Judy waited.

"How about Monday at 12:30pm?" asked the receptionist.

"Sorry, Monday doesn't suit me; I work full-time and my work doesn't finish until 5PM. Any possibility I could see him on another day or after 5pm?" asked Judy.

After looking at Fred's diary for few seconds the receptionist said, "No, that's the only time Fred is free. Or you'll have to wait another week."

"Ok, – well if that's the case, I will meet with him on Monday", confirmed Judy.

As she walked out of the school building, the same questions revolved in her head again. Is this school really the best place for Cameron? The school doesn't care if I have to take leave to see the Principal. Maybe they want to make it difficult for me to meet with him? Maybe Fred has directed his office staff to keep parents like me away!

As usual Cameron was quiet in the car and acted as if nothing had happened. "Can you tell me something, Cameron? What's happening this year? Why have you been misbehaving so much this year"? asked Judy.

Cameron's response was as usual, "I don't know".

It was Monday morning! The rest of the week had gone incident free. Judy was all prepared to talk to Fred about Cameron. She was not sure if she would be able to control her anger. Judy also knew if she wanted to keep Cameron in the same school then she needed to be calm and understanding.

Judy arrived at the school. As she walked towards reception, she could hear her heart thumping. It was not the best feeling. It felt as if she was going to have a war with the Principal. The receptionist knew that Judy had a meeting with the principal and asked her to wait for few minutes as he was on the phone.

Fred's initial gesture calmed Judy down. "I am going to make coffee for myself, Judy. What would you like, tea, coffee or I can offer you chilled water?" Fred had just come back from a Professional Development (PD) program on Positive Behaviour Support (PBS). He made a conscious effort to make Judy feel comfortable. Fred demonstrated two important skills of effective leaders – first he remembered the name of the parent and second he made her feel welcome.

"Judy, I know the reason you are here. Can I say that I am really sorry for what has happened this year with Cameron? We have had two other students who are going through similar issues. You may not know it but I was away for the last two weeks to undertake professional development in implementing a new whole school policy of PBS. All of my school staff will be undergoing training in PBS. I am keen that it is implemented throughout the school so that students like Cameron are engaged. Our focus within that will be the prevention of behavioural issues." Fred spoke enthusiastically.

He continued, "We will need strong support and the involvement of parents in making PBS a success in our school. We do want all parents to be informed of this new initiative and want to ensure that we work in close partnership with them."

Judy was a little more relaxed but was still keen to know why her son has been behaving so badly this year and asked why school had not been able to do anything about it. Fred said that it could have been a number of things, including that Cameron had been working with a new teacher and also with a new teacher aide. Judy was pleased to hear that Fred did seem to realise what she was suspecting: "Perhaps, Cynthia and the teacher aide have not understood Cameron really well. There could be a significant mismatch between the way Cameron is taught and the way he prefers to be taught. Or there could be another reason that we don't even know yet." Judy could hardly believe that Fred identified issues with the way the school was working with Cameron as the source of some of the problems. She had not expected to hear this in their meeting. Fred re-assured her that things could only improve from here. He told Judy that the school would be organizing professional development for all the school staff, including the teacher aides. He apologized for the lack of understanding that Cameron had received until now. But he then asked for her patience while sorting things out.

Next morning, Fred, informed the staff how excited he was after completing the PD on positive behaviour support. He also told the staff he was keen to insure that PBS was implemented in the school. To assist the school in implementation of the plan, Fred revealed he had asked Nick (staff already knew him) to conduct PD on the coming Friday.

"This will not be a one off PD, as we know that short term training has very limited impact, so I have asked Nick to work with us on an ongoing basis for the next six months. Nick will be running workshops for us on PBS. He will also be working one on one with some of us (if needed) to ensure that students like Cameron are fully included in our school." Cynthia sceptically commented: "I would really be interested to know what Nick can tell us that we don't already know about working with students like Cameron. I don't think our school is the best place for Cameron – he should go to the special school across the road."

Fred was quick to respond. "No, Cameron is not going anywhere. He will stay in our school and the litmus test for the success of our school is for Cameron and his mother to tell us how our school has been the best option for them. I know it is not easy, but I really want all of us to see that if we can do this for Cameron, not only will our school be a better place for Cameron, but for many other 'Camerons' we have not yet talked about. I can assure you, you will get all the necessary support for this to happen." Fred was all fired up. The staff could see a change in him since returning from the PD.

Nick arrived at the school on the curriculum day. The school was quiet with no students. Fred had already spoken to Nick about the level of some staff members' scepticism. This was nothing new for Nick. He knew that some educators would continue to offer instinctive resistance to change, but as the school started implementing the new policy, and as the rest of staff began to feel the impact of it, he really believed things would improve. Nick prepared well and always aimed at having something in his workshops that helped everyone feel relaxed. This day was no different. He began with a fun activity. Everyone was fully engaged in the activity and ready for the rest of the day.

Nick began, "As you know, I am here to talk about PBS. Today I will focus on two topics: working effectively with parents, and what teacher aides can do to implement PBS. I am sure you will agree that parents are important stakeholders in their children's education. If we can work at making sure parents are our partners in implementing any new policy, then the chances of its success can be increased manifold. I am not going to bombard you with lots of information. I will keep the session very simple. What I will do is identify the key principles of working effectively with parents, and then we will work in our small groups to find out how the principles can be translated into real life practice."

He showed the slide with four principles:

- Principle 1: Parents as partners
- Principle 2: Positive interaction
- Principle 3: Informed parents
- Principle 4: Capacity building for parents

Nick provided some examples to explain each of the four principles.

"Parents as partners means that we treat parents as equal partners in everything that we do in our school, rather than treating them as if they don't know anything. This will require a fundamental shift in the way we have worked with parents in the past. We may even think about what we can learn from them to improve the way we teach. Yes, I do mean it – we have to start treating them as if they too may have strategies we can use to work effectively with their child. We need to spend time with parents to find out about those strategies."

"Positive interaction will also mean a significant shift in the way we interact with parents. The current tendency has been that we contact parents only when their child misbehaves or breaks a rule. I am suggesting that we need to change this. We need to find ways that our interactions with parents are positive. We also need to make sure that we use modes of communication with parents that allow them to stay in close touch with us like emails. We need to think of ways we can welcome them into our classrooms and schools. Knowing and remembering the names of the parents is a very powerful strategy – not many parents expect us to remember their names, but when we do, they feel personally important, valued, and welcomed."

"'Informed parents' are those who know about various things that we are doing in our classrooms and in the school. For example, we would like our parents to know that our school is implementing whole school PBS. So we'd also like to give them opportunities to discuss what they could do to make it effective for their child. I have created a one-page summary about PBS in layman's terms that you may like to provide to parents. The summary provides basic information that parents need to know so that they are not overwhelmed with the information but at the same time they can see how it may affect their child in our school. I must say that there is strong evidence (Brough & Irvin, 2001; Henderson & Mapp, 2002; President's Commission on Excellent in Special Education, 2002) in support of keeping parents informed of schooling practices. Parents who are well informed of school practices connect well to the school. This also has the direct effect of their child feeling connected to the school. You can use the same principle of keeping parents informed of your curricular focus and teaching strategies, using different modes of communication with them. Fred has suggested that he will be very happy to organize parent meetings on a monthly basis so as to allow parents to come to school to have an informal chat with you about school activities most relevant to their child."

"The last principle is an important one. We want to work closely with parents to ensure that they acquire skills to interact positively with their children. We have identified two areas for parent training this term. These are resilience training and preventative discipline. The timing of the workshops in this term will coincide with the workshops that I will be running with school staff and students on both these topics. We are anticipating that this approach will allow us to see the impact at the whole school level, rather than just targeting one student and his or her family, or worse still, potentially just one teacher!"

"What we want to do for the next few hours is to come up with practical ways to make these principles part of our practice. We are expecting to have at least three to four practical ideas for translating the principle into practice. Well thought and practical ideas that you come up with will become part of the school policy. Fred has told me that he will find extra resources if there is such a need for the practices to be implemented."

Kate was enthusiastic to work on the task straightway. She collected some butcher paper for her group and they each started writing their ideas. Cynthia, who was also in Kate's group, came up with some great ideas. She said: "I am going to draft a letter for all parents of children in my class so that they know what I have been doing in my class. I will also be collecting emails from all my parents and making a list of parents to send an email to on a monthly basis. What I am thinking for parents like Judy (everyone in her group knew Judy) is that I might be writing an individual email to her on a more regular basis. I hope this will show her that I am keen to work with Cameron, and do want to see that he enjoys my class and is less disruptive in future."

All the groups presented their ideas. Nick compiled a list of possible practices that could be adopted to implement each of the four principles. Fred was pleased to see really useful strategies identified by his staff. He knew that now he had to find extra resources to enable certain necessary changes become possible. It was time for lunch break.

Questions for reflection

Think of the parent of a child with whom you have had most difficult interactions. Do you think you have used all four principles working with the parent(s)? Would you like to add another principle to this list? What and why?

Once you have done this, reconsider yourself as the parent of the most difficult student you have taught so far. What do you expect from the teacher(s)?

As soon as lunch was over, Nick was keen to make a start. The focus of the next session was on teacher aides. Nick put up a slide of a shoe and asked the participants to share something unique about the picture. Kate said that it was a big shoe and it wouldn't fit a child. Cynthia said that the colour of the shoe was unique (dark green). Nick has not yet got the answer for which he was searching! Kate suddenly said, "It has Velcro".

Nick replied, "Yes, spot on. This is what I wanted to hear. I will come back to it later but let's make a start. This morning we talked about what we need to do to work effectively with parents using the whole school PBS approach. What I want to do now is talk about how teacher aides should be working and how should we all be working with them within this approach. I am pleased to see that we have some teacher aides (pointing towards Narelle) in our session today. By the way, the focus of my presentation is not just teacher aides but everyone in the school workforce including teaching staff. We will do it the same way as we did this morning. I will identify the key principles of how teacher aides should be working within this framework, and we will then work in our small groups to come up with the practices for each principle".

Nick put up the next slide of the following principles:

• Principle 1: Team teaching
• Principle 2: Team player and partnership
• Principle 3: Capacity building

"Before moving into small groups, let's look at this slide again (shoe with a Velcro) to make sense of the Team teaching principle. Historically, and even now, this is how a teacher aide has worked with a student: We have a child who might have some behavioural issues (or a disability), we then get funding from the department and we employ a teacher (or integration) aide. The main role of the teacher aide is to work solely with that student. This approach is sometimes known as a Velcro approach to integration. In fact there are parents who would refuse to allow the teacher aide to be used for anything other than assisting their child, always and only with their child. If a child goes to the playground, the teacher aide is with him; when the child goes to toilet, the aide is with him. In many schools, teacher aides are employed to support inclusion of a student with a disability."

"In reality, this approach effectively slips into the social exclusion of a student. This happens because in order to receive support from a teacher aide, a student must first be labelled as having a disability (otherwise there is no funding). So what we have done for the student is to demonstrate something is wrong with him/her and that's why he/she needs the support of another person. Also, because the teacher aide is always with the student, peers tend to stay away from that student. This leads to reduced interaction between the student and important social networking with peers, and undermines the philosophy of inclusion, unnecessarily building barriers to social learning."

"What I am suggesting is that we move away from this old approach where the teacher aide is tied to working with one student, to one that allows the teacher aide to work alongside a small group of students. When the student (who is funded to receive support) needs any assistance, then the teacher aide can assist him or her. But there is no need for a teacher aide to be 'velcroed' to a student! There are clearly two benefits of this approach. First, we have an extra person in our class to assist with our teaching. Second, the student is not stigmatized as the one who needs constant assistance."

"I would like to share with you a research study that would further explain the points I just made. A group of researchers (Young, Simpson, Miles, & Kamps, 1997) undertook an observational study of three primary grade children who were attending inclusive classrooms. They found that teacher interactions with those students whose aides were not in close proximity to the students were more frequent compared to the students whose aides were in close proximity to them. Giangreco et al. (2005, p. 31) has also recorded similar observations:

.... busy teachers tend to work with other students when they know the student with a disability already has individual attention. ...The assignment of an individual para-professional to a student with a disability often co-occurs with lower levels of teacher engagement, whereas the use of a classroom paraprofessional, under the direction of the teacher, more often occurs with higher levels of teacher engagement

"The second principle is one that requires all of us to think differently about teacher aides. In my many years of experience in working in schools, I have noted that the teacher aides are treated as second-class citizens in our education system.

There is a tendency to regard teacher aides, being paid lower salaries to work with the most difficult, and sadly with less academic students in our schools, as 'not really teachers', and so often not receiving the same respect deserved and given to other members of our schooling community."

"There is also an implied belief that by providing a teacher aide for a student with disability in the classroom reduces a teacher's responsibility for that student. By the way, this is not a problem of one school or a school district; it is the problem of the whole educational system. We expect teacher aides to make instructional and curricular decisions about a student. The teacher aide becomes the main educator for the student and 'displaces' the qualified teacher. It needs to change. And changing it cannot happen unless we start believing that teacher aides are 'equal' members of our educational. The education of a student with a disability should not be seen as the sole responsibility of the teacher aide but it is a joint responsibility of both the teacher aide and the teacher."

"The need to improve the status of support staff is not easy. There are many occasions when a teacher aide may not have adequate skills and qualifications to work with students presenting a range of behavioural issues. The teacher aides are often asked to take a prominent role teaching students who are most difficult to teach. They take responsibility for roles for which they are often not well prepared (Giangreco et al., 2005). Building their capacity to be effective team members requires us to provide them with opportunities to undertake professional development. They should not just be learning about how to work with a student, but should also learn about the whole school policy. This is one of the reasons Fred has asked all teacher aides to be part of all PD activities."

In many ways we are in a fortunate position as Narelle is perhaps one of the well-qualified professionals with a Graduate Diploma in Special Education. We cannot ask for better-qualified teacher aides. However, we know that not all integration-aides will be as well qualified as Narelle. What I suggest we should do is to find out from people like Narelle what kind of PD activities would be good for them as well as for the rest of the school staff."

"What I would also like to suggest is, that rather than teacher aides to be on the receiving side of capacity building exercise, they take up an important role of delivering PDs for the staff. I know Narelle just completed a short course on "Motivation and engagement for difficult to teach students". It would be great (if you are ok with it) jf you could run a short session for us on how best we can apply what you learnt in the course."

Narelle's reaction was "No". "That's ok we can talk about this later", said Nick. "Any questions before we work in our small groups to operationalize the principles in our school's practices?"

Kate raised her hand and then commented, "It was a great session, Nick. There was a serious point of conflict for me until you raised the point about considering teacher aides as team players. To be very honest, I have always thought of teacher aides as 'helpers' in our class. What you just told me requires us to think completely differently about them, and I can clearly see the value of working with teacher aides as partners in our classrooms, rather than just as "velcroed helpers".

"That's great feedback, Kate," said Nick. "Can we work on the activity now?'

The participants then started working in their small groups. Many suggestions that came from the groups were quite impressive. For example James suggested, "we must talk to parents when they ask that a teacher aide should be assigned to their child only. If we know about parents' motivation then we can do something about it. My suspicion is that parents feel their son or daughter needs to be protected. However, they may not realize that such overprotection could alienate and isolate their child. Our group also thinks that we must speak to individual students who are allocated a teacher aide. We should find out from a student how he or she feels about having a teacher aide assigned to work with him or her solely, or if he or she would have better suggestions of how a teacher aide should be working in the school."

"Great suggestions, James" Nick commented. Others also shared some wonderful insights. Fred agreed, "Yes these are indeed great suggestions. I have to say I am impressed with everyone's active participation in the workshops today. I am looking forward to the action list compiled by Nick and will work on it as early as next week."

Questions for reflection

Think of a student with a severe behaviour problem in your class/ school. The student is assigned a full time aide.

Having understood that the Velcro approach may not be very useful, how would you use the teacher aide? What other resources do you consider necessary to support this student?

CHAPTER 9

LOOKING BACK

Teaching Learning on the Road

OVERVIEW AND KEY CONCEPTS

- Conclusion: implications for the ongoing journey
- Reflecting upon experience: perspectives and practice
- Putting Theory to work: sustaining positive learning
- Staying positive: including, involving, & innovating

CONCLUSION: IMPLICATIONS FOR THE ONGOING JOURNEY?

At the beginning of this book we talked about learning teaching on the road. The idea of the road trip has been used as a structuring device to organize a series of accounts, perspectives and events describing the journey of working in education. In a sense we have tried to teach teaching as part of the journey, learning on the road. We hope that by meeting several characters on this journey you have recognized a great deal through being able to identify in a practical and applied sense with the characters while also sporting a healthy sense of critical evaluation where you have found yourself occasionally disagreeing with some of the ideas and opinions expressed.

We have not introduced a radical theory or new ways of thinking about the work of learning and success in teaching. What we do hope is to have presented several different approaches which are practical as well as underpinned by validated theory. At the same time, we hope we have demonstrated that the role of the practitioner developing one's praxis requires both critical reflection and problem-solving thinking in an applied mix of theory and practice. To this end, we do claim that '*positive approaches*' to the work of learning and teaching will ultimately and simultaneously benefit teachers, students, parents, and the full range of other members that make up the school community.

Furthermore, we think there is in the detail recounted in these stories signposts to discovering yet more to reflect upon, including some key principles, ideas or values you have witnessed while on the road trip. We hope these will serve to help you reflect and think about your own practice, develop praxis as knowledge and expertise, and encourage you to talk with peers about these ideas, beliefs and underlying values. For the most part, you will doubtlessly seek to do this in order to confirm better ways of working, facilitated by clearer ideas of learning and teaching, and so find fresh ways and means for educating our individual students. In all of this we expect that the theories of humanistic and positive psychology will illuminate the places, people and contexts described on the road trip. We do claim, too, and ask that you reflect upon this claim, that this account brings a new practical and significant meaning to *being positive about contributing to the learning environment.*

All in all, however, while the use of reflection is central to our approach, we suggest that adopting at the same time a parallel 'hard-headed' problem-posing critical evaluation is crucial to maintaining momentum and making headway along the road. It is, as we stated at the end of the first chapter, very much like learning how to drive, or to drive better, which quite critically means using the rear vision mirror. The driver makes full use of the running reflection in the mirror, checking on what has passed, in order to take running decisions about the present, so that the journey may continue and a destination at some point in the near future be safely reached. And the good news here is that while you may reach more than one stop-over, you will not reach the final destination. While this chapter concludes with a specific part of the journey, there is more to come. So it is now timely to re-emphasize another opinion, closely related to the belief that as a professional, a practitioner, and/or an expert teacher, none of us ever stop learning!

The truth is, and we use this word deliberately, looking back on the account in this book, characters learn and rehearse the skills, attitudes and understandings that make up successful teaching and learning. Kate, Fred, Cynthia, and Nick, all at differing points in their career, share similar professional needs in terms of seeking clarity in purpose and intention for their school community. And crucially, they individually feel some ownership of that community. Eleanor takes on a huge task, at the start of a new post, and she manages to both facilitate as well as experience a seismic shift in personal learning. Confidence grows and so too does success. And what is equally important to understand, this kind of learning is just as relevant for students engaged in classroom activity as it is for their teachers.

Many colleagues and students, however, who feel alienated or displaced, often struggle to find a personal affiliation or identification with the corporate enterprise that is embodied in belonging to a learning community. They need to be further supported in developing and continuously using new knowledge in a way that fosters positive behavior. The learning can be formal and informal, is both personal and social, and so inevitably includes others in the school community. In this sense, learning leadership for the professional involves a range of actions and activities which make up far more than instructional leadership; it embodies a range of various contributions to the learning organization which are actually about leadership, leading and enabling change that will inevitably shape and /or structure the successful school community (see, for example, the leadership for learning centre at Cambridge University in the UK at http://www.educ.cam.ac.uk/research/academicgroups/leadinglearning/).

REFLECTING UPON EXPERIENCE: PERSPECTIVES AND PRACTICE

Perhaps at this late point in this book there is a need to focus a little more closely on the *benefits* claimed as outcomes at various points covered in this book. If we imagine, for a moment or three, an Educational/School Psychologist (EP) called Nick, a Teacher/Educator called Kate, and a PD Consultant in Educational Management called Sam, sitting around the coffee table. The question of positive learning and using psychology in education has been raised. The discussion reflects in turn many of the accounts presented in the central part of this book.

Nick, the EP, takes a lead in the discussion, as he regards himself as a bit of an expert on learning and the psychology most relevant to success and reward in the work place (as well as for life more generally). What Nick insists is that *positive psychology* can teach all of us how to opt out of a series of transactional games we have learned to play that get in the way of learning and personal development. There is a need, Nick argues, for deliberately encouraging grown up 'adult skills' in assertiveness rather than a child-like negative use of aggression or destructive expression of anger. The latter can so easily create dysfunctional victim-perpetrator interactions between people. Instead of sustaining negative attributions for our weaknesses and disappointments, often involving the blaming of others and harsh criticism of perceived failure or poor performance, we need to look more deeply at what is going on in the inter-personal relations being played out in the classroom, and beyond in other areas of the school community. Nick maintains we need to opt in by taking more self-orientated responsibility for our own person, while accepting others in their search for self-actualization. We need to play the ball, not the person. We need to work harder at listening attentively.

The benefits of adopting this theory, Nick argues, makes for better, more grounded individuals and a clearer more open exchange between peers; teachers with parents, and students with teachers, in the classroom. In terms of an inclusive and authentic approach to educational diversity, this philosophy will yield a number of benefits reflecting mutual respect and at its best, unconditional regard that facilitates a parity or equality of esteem for minority groups, students with differences associated with learning difficulties or problems with mental health. All of this, Nick argues, is in turn reinforced by the benefit of nurturing positive attitudes toward perceptions of self-efficacy, and the range of self-monitoring tactics we can learn in engendering emotional resilience, affirmation, well-being and serial fulfillment. In fact, in many respects, this is about learning how to be OK with being happy! Nick concludes by emphasizing the view point that the greater the levels of engagement and affiliation experienced by everyone involved in the school community, the more healthy and vibrant the learning experience.

Kate speaks up next, accepting all that had been stated but wishing to represent it as part of a differing perspective on the work of the teacher associated with professional learning and teacher education. This, she seems to argue, is and always should be, regarded as an essential part of the 'learning game'. It is vital, she adds, that teachers continue while 'on the road', that is, throughout their career, to be reflective, thinking practitioners – asking from time to time basic soul-searching questions like 'why am I a teacher?' and 'how do I know that what I am doing is the best for the student?'. She cites Dewey as a must read (Dewey, 1933), and Loughran (2010) as a more recent catch-up read.

What is more, Kate continues, teachers need to translate this approach into practical strategies for the classroom. In terms of constructing *positive learning environments,* she stresses the important place of prevention, particularly in learning and using new teaching strategies for creating a classroom environment where a student will not need to be disruptive. This for Kate practically speaking, meant putting the theory into application and answering the age-old $64k question of theory, that is, 'so what'? Developing approaches such as cooperative learning, peer-based learning groups, and opportunities for personal styles-based differentiation were perhaps three of several useful methods to be applied and developed in what she hoped might be called the 'inclusive classroom'.

"Then next is the task of re-applying Nick's psychology", added Kate. "The key concerns always addressed by effective teachers are an awareness of student interest and motivation,, and the trick of using both to nurture emotional resilience and/ or perseverance as key traits in their learning behaviour. A truly effective teacher also works at combining this with a readiness to learn, to take emotional risks, to engage in the tasks designed by the teacher. For those children experiencing social, emotional and behavioural difficulties, this approach is reinforced by a third special pedagogic tactic, aimed at providing restorative experiences in the design of learning tasks, as well as a more proscribed skills-based development.

"It is", Kate suggests, "the kind of approach embodied in the recent provision typified by the nurture group in primary education" (see http://www.nurturegroups.org).

Again, the emphasis for Kate was not only one of accepting individual differences across the school student population in terms of personality, capability and performance, but also the different expression and need for seeking affiliation, engagement and enhancement through the work of personal and social connections. This also needed especially to be considered in any relationships with significant other(s), linked to membership of the school community. Ideally, it is 'cool' to belong to the class, to the school, and to turn up for the start of the school week. It is a good place to be, even if teenagers / peers at any point do not always easily admit it in the same working week! But here is the thing – one day it MIGHT VERY WELL be 'cool' even to admit it!

Sam, the consultant nodded his head. Nothing wrong with all of this except it has to be woven into an organized and managed form of educational provision. Absolutely crucial was the realization, for Sam, that the learning wasn't simply thought to be located in the classroom. It embraced every aspect of the school community. Secondly, Sam wanted to confront the whole idea of educational inclusion. He was searching for a better way of tackling this issue that was not simply an idealistic imperative that inevitably failed in the learning context. This failure seemed to him to occur in several different ways but especially when the going got tough. Educating students, all students, needed to involve more for Sam than the idea of an inclusive ideal that amounted to saying here is a straightforward offer of 'access to the watering hole', 'drink if you wish' or 'just go away'.

This appropriate and desired drinking (learning) at the water-hole (formal school setting) inevitably and very often in a dramatic manner, simply did not happen when for example a disruptive or harmful behaviour occurred in the school day. Sam used to call serious misbehavior or the disturbed and dangerous (double-D) student, the 'Achilles Heel' of the school inclusion lobby. At its most extreme, this behaviour involved risk to life, at its most irritating, risk to property. A school principal needed to be able to exclude a student for reasons of protection and clearly stated regard for health and safety.

"Nevertheless", Sam concluded, "a positive approach to leadership distributed throughout the school community is a second level rejoinder for what Kate had described as *positive behavior management.*"

"Distributing leadership opportunities and opportunities for individuals to take up the chance to manage and adapt", added Sam, "are crucial ingredients in an approach embodying *positive behavior management.*"

"At the same time," Sam exclaimed, "it also seems to be a mechanism for facilitating community member engagement within any organization in decision-making, strategic planning and change management". It is about maximizing the ideas that could be found in Glasser's 'choice theory' (e.g., at http://www.choicetheory.com). Equally importantly, it offers ideas, tactics, and a method for a psycho educational model of pedagogy that carries with it the potential benefits of cognitive behaviour processes that relate to spoken therapies and restorative education.

Sam remembered reading how Cynthia had introduced choice theory into her classroom. Great! But it needs to ripple outwards beyond the classroom. "The first golden principle in educational leadership, Sam claimed, "should remain implementing a whole-school approach to learning, teaching and development. Think school community, better still, think learning community."

"What is more," Sam added, "the use of a transforming model of leadership necessarily involves issues of social justice, moral values, and more reinforcing work aimed at developing an institutional resilience equivalent to, and perhaps a reflection of, individual resilience, in the members of its community."

This required a form of inclusive leadership concerned with growing what Sam liked to call the aspirational dream of a consensual community. For Sam, there was a desperate need to develop a new and perhaps more intelligent, smart, even savvy and pragmatic approach to educational diversity, perhaps moving away from the past in terms of a reliance upon labeling categories such as special educational needs, disability, ethnic discrimination or disadvantage, to begin re-thinking an approach that more decisively reflects universal design in the curriculum, and the meeting of individual and personal learning needs in one or more new ways. Sam anticipated these developments as using new contextualized 'authentic' or 'dynamic' forms of assessment, as well as other established tests for individual differences in the psychologist's toolbox, but with increasing acknowledgement and acceptance of personal and social diversity.

"Most importantly," Sam said, I'd want to see pedagogic and curricular developments reflecting something I would suggest might be called 'intelligent inclusion'". He wanted to introduce a renewed emphasis upon a comprehensive approach to education that did not select students from the outset but rather did consider individual differences throughout the 'cradle to grave' educational experience.

"This might," Sam continued, "be provided for in the idea of a learning village or community that integrates several forms of social, health and educational provision". Creating 'joined-up' services was one way to plan provision intelligently or even just sensibly, albeit for Sam, this most certainly did not mean re-instating a comprehensive ideal in which 'one size will fit all' as the approach to inclusion. It also meant developing fresh approaches to ensure new required ways of inter-agency working could be successfully managed.

"After all," Sam opined, "we are all learners engaged in learning even though we are teachers!" The three ended by agreeing they should write a book!

PUTTING THEORY TO WORK: SUSTAINING POSITIVE LEARNING

Taking this discussion a little further brings us around to looking back again at the various voices used within the different narratives in this book. We can see that all of the issues raised in the previous cameo are to be found being played out at various points in the careers of the main characters. Their story is one of putting theory to work.

The long game, however, is one of creating and sustaining positive learning in every aspect of the school organization. We see, for example, positive behaviour support in Tracy's account of managing Tom in the classroom. In a similar way, full accounts of adopting reflective teaching and using positive psychology are visible in Cynthia's story, and involves maximizing choice in her teaching and learning.

The classroom is the main context for this activity, and the scene of action, but the work also involves moving beyond the classroom. It involves parents as well as the teacher aide, and arguably may well involve others such as an educational / school psychologist, a social worker, and potentially even a baker who has successfully run a business for forty years. At some point perhaps, Tom will gain valuable work experience in such a bakery as part of his on-going education.

Further examples of putting this theory into practice and sustaining positive learning occur throughout the book. It is perhaps worth mentioning how similar is Kate's story of a new stage in her career at the beginning of the book, to Fred's start as the principal in a failing city school later in the book. One character is very new to the learning game and the road trip, the other much more experienced. Yet their feelings, thoughts and anticipation are not immediately or obviously that different. Both share the same kinds of challenges. Maintaining a positive approach to the task in hand for Kate is managing the sassy feedback of three students at the school gates in her first week at work; for Fred, it is resisting the urge to disappear into the distance instead of turning right in to the school driveway on his first day in the new job.

Finally, people like Eleanor and Fred display examples of what we might call 'intelligent inclusion' and 'transformative leadership'; in turn, they mobilize and engage the various members of the leadership groups to facilitate strategic growth in the school community (see Rayner, 2007, Shields, 2011 for more on these kinds of approaches to educational leadership). Eleanor takes up a lead role in facilitating policy development. She is new to this responsibility but sustains a shared approach to owning the work. The leadership group represents an example of how distributive leadership can work. The idea that a group representing a community of practice can form and re-form, and informally take up change is helpfully detailed by Wenger (2002), but the implications of situated cognition that form part of an organizational structure and shaping leadership is perhaps better described by Gronn (2000, 2002) and Spillane and Diamond (2007).

Furthermore, Fred in turn demonstrates how, as the school principal, applying this notion of distributed leadership can be blended with the idea of transformative leadership, and used to construct a way of 'growing' and/or 're-growing' organizational culture for an educational enterprise. The benefits of this approach are that it offers ways of assuring medium term development. It prevents a short term 'win-win', 'use it' and 'lose it', approach to change and work, which for Fred, is anathema to learning and educational development. It also has the added advantage of linking directly with the educationist's concern for inclusion. This in turn connects with social justice, access, empowerment, and equity issues; stuff that matters when we hope that education will be an opportunity for all, and serves the public good as well as facilitates personal development.

STAYING POSITIVE: INCLUDING, INVOLVING AND INNOVATING

Sometimes life is difficult and work as an educationist can appear tiring, thankless, and quite frankly so bad you feel like giving it all up. This is likely how Rob was feeling in chapter 2 after receiving 'supportive help' from the school principal. The first thing to remember is like it or not, you are one of many feeling this way and it is a fairly safe bet that someone else is feeling the same way right now. Furthermore, we have all experienced times like this when success is not so obvious, and failure seems all-enveloping.

A colleague (school psychologist) once said to us in conversation that he worked tirelessly at being a 'pathological optimist'. I am not sure if he succeeded, but what he did believe in were many of the ideas and values associated with positive psychology. The trick is to take perspective, if possible share the perspective with a friend, a trusted other, and reflect and evaluate together. It is useful too if at all possible to refer to and manage Seligman's three P's of pessimism (Seligman, 1975; 1998), and, to perhaps put this list up on a mental whiteboard so as to reflect upon its role in learning and teaching (our own and others). These Ps are:

- *Personalization* – that is – typical and persistent forms of internal dialogue which can often firstly go something like, 'I am responsible, totally to blame, for all the bad things that happen to me'. Or secondly, if something ever goes right, it is then simply 'a matter of good luck and nothing at all to do with me or my effort'; and, thirdly, 'I always suspect that any negative comment is immediately about me rather than the situation'. I am always to blame.
- *Permanence* – that is, a tendency for you to generalize, usually in a way that says something like "I'll *never* be able to do this." Or "Mr Smith is *always* annoying me." The key give away words in this internal dialogue are 'always' and/or 'never' which undermine a positive attitude to difficulty and/or challenge.
- *Pervasiveness* – that is – when a setback happens, it is an opening of the floodgate and our whole world is threatened with disaster. *Everything* is going to fail or fall, just like a row of dominos collapsing in a line. If one thing goes wrong, then it impacts every other aspect of your life. A good example is how we react to small things that suddenly loom large, like burning the toast for breakfast. From then on you are in a pessimistic, '*everything* is going to run badly' mood for the rest of the day, that impacts your work, your relationships and your overall sense of wellbeing.

The colleague just mentioned did stay positive most of the time while tackling some very difficult and challenging tasks. There is a distinct probability he had read quite a lot of Seligman's work. His enthusiasm for a task in hand was infectious, just as were his levels of commitment and perseverance. What he needed, sometimes, however, was a steer and a reminder that not everyone possessed his well-established optimism or his levels of personal drive. He needed to work at taking people with him.

The same principles hold true for *managing positive behavior* in the school context or classroom. Much as we may at times feel otherwise, student behavior is rarely a singularly ring-fenced, once only, dedicated mission to disrupt or destroy a teacher's lesson or status, or outlook on the profession'. A student's behavior will carry across contexts, places and even with very different people. The issue of difficult or problem behaviour is one best met and managed as a group where there is a common and agreed understanding of approach. School policy works best if it energizes practices that are largely preventive and/or restorative. This requires professional trust, as colleagues acknowledge difficulties and build ways of working together for a resolution. Nonetheless, often the problem can become an intense one to which an individual teacher needs to respond; yet the same principles stand. Share the problem, if not immediately, soon after, and hopefully, a team can work together to support and share in mediating the problem. Sharing a problem is not the same as 'not owning' it. Indeed it invariably reflects the very opposite: sharing is facilitative of problem ownership.

It is important to recognize that it is easier to fail or fall as a lone teacher than it is when you work as a member of a larger group, especially where that group has developed trust and coherence and established good team-work. Including and enabling the problem student is more often than not best dealt with by recognizing that the problem is not only, or very often not at all, simply about the student. As Nick, the School Psych stated earlier in this chapter, we do need to 'play the ball'. But while we play as an individual, we remain and play as part of a team. It is often the case that when a pupil has reacted inappropriately to the situation, and has triggered a series of actions or events that climax in a serious problem, the issue will finally be tackled by a number of professionals. The hope is that this group of practitioners will form part of a team. It is not always the case. An emphasis upon collaborative method, however, is not meant to understate the importance and impact of the individual working well or remaining a firm and fair teacher, and the importance of working to develop personal skills as part of the team-based approach of positive management.

Remember how Kate realized this shortly after negotiating an early encounter of the negative kind with her young niece and struggling to attentively listen? We all need to improve our skill in personal relations and use this in our professional practice. Nevertheless, while much of what we do as an educationist is about how we do it as an individual, united, working as a team, we will more often and more easily stand firm, get better results, and all in all have a better chance of sustaining a worthwhile and inclusive learning environment. Managing positive behavior in school is ultimately a team game.

Finally, we want to say that we each hope you will continue to enjoy journeying along the road trip 'learning to teach'. It may well be that we decide there is more of the journey we can share with you in the future. We hope you will share some of your own experiences, reflections, insights and new knowledge with colleagues, peers and students in your own place of work.

REFERENCES

Argyris, C. (1990). *Overcoming organisational defences*. Boston, MA: Allyn and Bacon.

Bandura, A. (1994). Self-efficacy. In V. S. Ramachaudran (Ed.), *Encyclopedia of human behavior* (Vol. 4, pp. 71–81). New York, NY: Academic Press. Retrieved from http://des.emory.edu/mfp/BanEncy.html

Bannigan, K., & Moores, A. (2009). A model of professional thinking: Integrating reflective practice and evidence based practice. *Canadian Journal of Occupational Therapy, 76*(5), 342–350.

Baud, D., & Walker, D. (1998). Promoting reflection in professional courses: The challenge of context. *Studies in Higher Education, 23*, 191–206.

Baxter Magolda, M. B. (2004). Evolution of a constructivist conceptualization of epistemological reflection. *Educational Psychologist, 39*, 31–42.

Bernstein, R. J. (1983). *Beyond objectivism and relativism*. Oxford, England: Blackwell.

Boody, R. M. (2008). Teacher reflection as teacher change, and teacher change as moral response. *Education, 128*(3), 498–506.

Brooks, S. R., Freiburger, S. M., & Grotheer, D. R. (1998). *Improving elementary student engagement in the learning process through integrated thematic instruction* (Unpublished master's thesis). Chicago, IL: Saint Xavier University. (ERIC Document Reproduction Service No. ED 421 274)

Brough, J. A., & Irvin, J. L. (2001). Parental involvement supports academic improvement among middle schoolers. *Middle School Journal, 32*(5), 56–61.

Brown, D. F, (1992). *The development of strategic classrooms in two secondary schools*. Waikanae, New Zealand: Wordsmiths.

Christensen, L. (2004). Through the looking glass: Reflection or refraction? Do you see what I see. *Journal of Social Studies Research, 28*(1), 33–46.

Csikszentmihalyi, M. (1990). *Flow: The psychology of optimal experience*. New York, NY: Harper Collins Publishers.

Daniel, B., & Wassell, S. (2002). *The school years: Assessing and promoting resilience in vulnerable children 2*. London, England: Jessica Kingsley Publishers.

Daniels, H., & Cole, T. (2010). Exclusion from school: Short-term setback or a long term of difficulties? *European Journal of Special Needs Education, 25*(2), 115–130.

Dev, P. C. (1997). Intrinsic motivation and academic achievement: What does their relationship imply for classroom teacher? *Remedial and Special Education, 18*(1), 12–19.

Dewey, J. (1933). *How we think: A restatement of the relation of reflective thinking to education process*. Boston, MA: Heath.

Dinkmeyer, D., & Dreikurs, R. (2000). *Encouraging children to learn* (Reprint ed.). Sussex, England: Brunner-Routledge.

Galton, F. (1865). Hereditary talent and character. *Macmillan's Magazine, 12*, 157–166.

Garmon, M. A. (2005). Six key factors changing preservice teachers' attitudes/beliefs about diversity. *Educational Studies, 38*(3), 275–286.

Giangreco, M. F., Yuan, S., McKenzie, B., Cameron, P., & Fialka, J. (2005). "Be careful what you wish for": Five reasons to be concerned about the assignment of individual paraprofessional. *Teaching Exceptional Children, 37*(5), 28–34.

Glasser, W. (2007). The Glasser quality school: A combination of choice theory and the competence-based classroom. *Journal of Adventist Education, 69*(3), 4–9.

Grant, C. A., & Zeichner, K. M. (1984). On becoming a reflective teacher. In C. A. Grant (Ed.), *Preparing for reflective teaching*. Boston, MA: Allyn & Bacon.

Grimley, M., Morris, S., Rayner, S., & Riding, R. (2004). Supporting school improvement: The development of a scale for assessing pupils' emotional and behavioural development. *Assessment in Education, 11*(3), 273–300.

Gronn, P. (2000). Distributed properties: A new architecture for leadership. *Educational Management and Administration, 28*, 317–338.

REFERENCES

Gronn, P. (2002). Distributed leadership as a unit of analysis. *The Leadership Quarterly, 13*, 423–451.

Guay, F., Chanal, J., Ratelle, C. F., Marsh, H. W., Larose, S., & Boivin, M. (2010). Intrinsic, identified, and controlled types of motivation for school subjects in young elementary school children. *British Journal of Educational Psychology, 80*(4), 711–735.

Harvey, J., & Delfabbro, P. H. (2004). Psychological resilience in disadvantaged youth: A critical review. *Australian Psychologist, 39*(1), 3–13.

Henderson, A. T., & Mapp, K. L. (2002). *A new wave of evidence: The impact of school, family, and community connections on student achievement.* Austin, TX: Southwest Educational Development Laboratory, National Center for Family & Community Connections with Schools. Retrieved May 25, 2005, from http://www.sedl.org/connections/resources/evidence.pdf

Jacobson, P. (2002, Winter). What it takes to be an effective leader. *Canadian Manager.*

Jay, J. K., & Johnson, K. L. (2002). Capturing complexity: A typology of reflective practice for teacher education. *Teaching and Teacher Education, 18*, 73–85.

Johnson, D. W., & Johnson, R. T. (1999). *Learning together and alone: Cooperative, competitive, and individualistic learning.* Boston, MA: Allyn & Bacon.

Johnson, D. W., Johnson, R. T., & Stanne, M. B. (2000). *Cooperative learning methods: A meta-analysis.* Retrieved May 23, 2011, from http://www.cooperation.org/pages/cl-methods.html

Klem, A. M., & Connell, J. P. (2004). Relationships matter: Linking teacher support to student engagement and achievement. *Journal of School Health, 74*, 262–273.

Lai, E. R. (2011). Motivation: A literature review. *Always Learning Pearson*, pp. 1–44.

Larrivee, B. (2000). Transforming training practice: Becoming the critically reflective teacher. *Reflective Practice, 1*(3), 293–307.

Loughran, J. J. (2002). Effective reflective practice: In search of meaning in learning about teaching. *Journal of Teacher Education, 53*(1), 33–43.

Loughran, J. J. (2010). *What expert teachers do: Teachers' professional knowledge of classroom practice.* Sydney, Australia & London, England: Allen & Unwin, Routledge.

Lumsden, L. S. (1994). *Student motivation to learn* (ERIC Digest No. 92). Eugene, OR: ERIC Clearinghouse on Educational Management. (ERIC Document Reproduction Service No. ED 370 200)

Maslow, A. (1954). *Motivation and personality.* New York, NY: Harper and Row.

Masten, A. S., & Coatsworth, J. D. (1998). The development of competence in favourable and unfavourable environments: Lessons from research on successful children. *American Psychologist, 53*, 205–220.

Mastropieri, M. A., & Scruggs, T. E. (2010). *The inclusive classroom: Strategies for effective instruction* (4th ed.). Upper Saddle River, NJ: Prentice Hall.

McGrew, K. S. (2009). CHC theory and the human cognitive abilities project: Standing on the shoulders of the giants of psychometric intelligence research. *Intelligence, 37*, 1–10.

Mezirow, J. (1997). Transformative learning: Theory to practice. *New Directions for Adult and Continuing Education, 74*, 5–12.

Mezirow, J., Taylor, E., & Associates. (Eds.). (2009). *Transforming learning into practice.* San Francisco, CA: Jossey-Bass.

Monahan, K. C., Oesterle, S., & Hawkins, J. D. (2010). Predictors and consequences of school connectedness: The case for prevention. *The Prevention Researcher, 17*(3), 3–6.

Muis, K. R. (2007). The role of epistemic beliefs in self-regulated learning. *Educational Psychologist, 42*(3), 173–190.

NCH. (2007). *Literature review: Resilience in children and young people.* London, England: Children's Charity.

Peterson, C., & Seligman, M. E. P. (2004). *Character strengths and virtues: A handbook and classification.* Oxford, England: Oxford University Press.

Pirsig, R. (2006). *Zen and the art of motorcycle maintenance.* New York, NY: HarperTorch.

Poutiatine, M. I. (2009). What is transformation? Nine principles toward an understanding transformational process for transformational leadership. *Journal of Transformative Education, 7*(3), 189–208.

President's Commission on Excellence in Special Education. (2002). *A new era: Revitalizing special education for children and their families*. Retrieved May 26, 2005, from http://www.ed.gov/inits/commissionsboards/whspecialeducation/reports/index.html

Qualifications and Curriculum Authority. (2001). *Supporting school improvement: Emotional and behavioural development*. London, England: Qualifications and Curriculum Authority.

Rayner, S. (2007). *Managing special and inclusive education*. London, England: Sage.

Rayner, S. (2009). Educational diversity and learning leadership: A proposition, some principles and a model of inclusive leadership? *Educational Review, 61*(4), 433–447.

Rayner, S. (2011). *Managing educational diversity: Developing transformative leadership and professional praxis in the 21st Century learning community*. In C. Shields (Ed.), *Transformative leadership reader*. New York, NY: Peter Lang Publishing.

Redl, F., & Wineman, D. (1957). *The aggressive child*. Glencoe, IL: Free Press.

Rigby, K. (2001). *Stop the bullying: A handbook for schools*. Melbourne, Australia: Australian Council for Educational Research.

Robbins, B. D (2008). What is the good life? Positive psychology and the renaissance of humanistic psychology. *The Humanistic Psychologist, 36*(2), 96–112.

Rogers, B. (1998). *You know the fair rule* (2nd ed.). London, England: Pitman Publishing.

Rogers, B. (2000). *Classroom behaviour: A practical guide to effective teaching behaviour management and colleague support*. London, England: Pitman Publishing.

Rogers, B. (2003). *Cracking the hard class: Strategies for managing the harder than average class*. London, England: Pitman Publishing.

Rogers, C. (1969). *Freedom to learn: A view of what education might become* (1st ed.). Columbus, OH: Charles Merill.

Scheffler, I. (1968). University scholarship and the education of teachers. *Teacher College Record, 70*(1), 1–12.

Seligman, M. E. P. (1975). *Helplessness: On depression, development, and death*. San Francisco, CA: W.H. Freeman.

Seligman, M. E. P. (1998). *Learned optimism*. New York, NY: Simon & Schuster Inc.

Seligman, M. E. P. (2002). *Authentic happiness: Using the new positive psychology to realize your potential for lasting fulfilment*. New York, NY: Free Press.

Sharma, U., & Loreman, T. (2014). Teacher educator perspectives on systemic barriers to inclusive education: An international conversation. In P. Jones (Ed.), *Insider perspective on inclusive education* (pp. 168–177). New York, NY: Routledge.

Sharma, U., & Nuttal, A. (2015). The impact of training on pre-service teacher attitudes, concerns and efficacy toward inclusion. *Asia-Pacific Journal of Teacher Education*. doi:10.1080/1359866X.2015.1081672

Sharma, U., Simi, J., & Forlin, C. (2015). Preparedness of pre-service teachers for inclusive education in the Solomon Islands. *Australian Journal of Teacher Education, 40*(5), 103–116.

Shields, C. M. (2010). Leadership: Transformative. In P. Peterson, E. Baker, & B. McGraw (Eds.), *International encyclopaedia of education* (Vol. 5, pp. 26–33). Oxford, England: Elsevier.

Shields, C. M. (Ed.). (2011). *Transformative leadership: A reader*. New York, NY: Peter Lang Publishing.

Slavin, R. E. (1995). *Cooperative learning: Theory, research, and practice*. Needham Heights, MA: Allyn & Bacon.

Sparks-Langer, G. M., Simmons, J. M., Pasch, M., Colton, A., & Starko, A. (1990). Reflective pedagogical thinking: How can we promote it and measure it. *Journal of Teacher Education, 41*(4), 23–32.

Spillane, J., & Diamond, J. B. (2007). (Eds.). *Distributed leadership in practice*. New York, NY: Teachers College Press.

Stacey, R. D. (1992). *Managing the unknowable: Strategic boundaries between order and chaos in organizations*. San Francisco, CA: Jossey-Bass.

Stacey, R. D. (1993). *Strategic management and organizational dynamics*. London, England: Pitman.

Tuckman, B. (1965). Developmental sequence in small groups. *Psychological Bulletin, 3*(6), 384–399.

Valli, L. (1997). Listening to other voices: A description of teacher reflection in the United States. *Peabody Journal of Education, 72*(1), 67–88.

REFERENCES

Wenger, E., McDermott, R., & Snyder, W. (2002). *Cultivating communities of practice*. Boston, MA: Harvard Business School.

Young, B., Simpson, R., Myles, B. S., & Kamps, D. M. (1997). An examination of paraprofessional involvement in supporting students with autism. *Focus on Autism and Other Developmental Disabilities, 12*(1), 31–38, 48.

Zeichner, K. M., & Liston, D. P. (1996). *Reflective teaching: An introduction*. Mahwah, NJ: Lawrence Erlbaum Associates.

ABOUT THE AUTHORS

Umesh Sharma, PhD (Melb), MAPS, born in India is a special educator and educational psychologist. He has taught in special and regular schools in India and Australia. He joined Monash University in 2002 as a lecturer. He is now an Associate Professor and leads programs in special education within the faculty. He is leading a number of research projects in over 20 countries (including China, Bangladesh, India, Fiji, Solomon Islands) that target inclusion of children with diversities into mainstream schools and communities. His research interests include inclusive teaching strategies, measuring attitude and teaching efficacy, and positive behaviour support. He continues to enjoy cricket on field and on screen.

John Roodenburg, PhD (Melb) FAPS MCEDP, born in The Netherlands, is an Australian Teacher, and Psychologist. Married to another teacher and psychologist Esther, and with five adult children, he spent over thirty years as a practitioner before coming to the Faculty of Education at Monash University where he is now a Senior Lecturer and Course Leader for Postgraduate Educational and Developmental Psychology. He is currently National Chair of the Australian Psychological Society College of Educational and Developmental Psychologists. His passions include thinking styles, grandchildren, roasting coffee, and Christian spirituality.

Stephen Rayner, PhD (Birmingham University), is Dean of Education, Newman University, UK. He was formerly Head teacher of Penwithen School (Dorset LEA) and had previously taught in secondary and special education before this and moving to the School of Education at the University of Birmingham. He more recently worked as a Professor of Education, firstly at the University of Gloucestershire, and then, Oxford Brookes University, UK. He led both PGR and Research as Director of Studies in schools of education at these Universities over the last twenty years. He is now also Director of the Newman Institute of Leadership in Education [NILE]. Interests and scholarship still lie with understanding individuality and the self in learning, teaching, leadership and managing education, as well as drinking coffee.

CPSIA information can be obtained at www.ICGtesting.com
Printed in the USA
BVOW06*0838030616

450538BV00001B/2/P